Dear Ms Smith,

I have read the book 'Mothers and Sons' and I want to thank you with all my heart for writing it. It has lifted an incredible burden off me—I carried the guilt for 35 years. I thought something was terribly wrong with me. Sometimes I wished we would all die, then none of it would matter. But now I see there are millions like me—mothers who love their sons. So I'm not crazy! I'm on nearly every page—and from page 20 onwards I think you wrote it just for me.

Now I give you my grateful thanks because it has eased my sadness and fear—and unbearable pain. I'm really ashamed of all this—so please don't tell that I wrote, or say my name. My son lives in New York and his wife is American, and I'm nothing to the baby—hey, this was only going to be a thank you note—not a sad story of how I miss my boy.

God bless you.

Other books by this author

A cargo of women: Susannah Watson and the Convicts of the *Princess Royal*
A cargo of women: the novel

Mothers and Sons

Babette Smith

ALLEN & UNWIN

First edition 1995
This impression published in 1996 by
Allen & Unwin Pty Ltd
9 Atchison Street, St Leonards, NSW 2065 Australia
Phone: (61 2) 9901 4088
Fax: (61 2) 9906 2218
E-mail: 100252.103@compuserve.com

National Library of Australia
Cataloguing–in–Publication entry:

Smith, Babette, 1942– .
Mothers and sons.

Bibliography.
ISBN 1 86448 222 2.

1. Mothers and sons—Australia. 2. Mothers and sons—Great Britain.
3. Masculinity (Psychology). I. Title.

306.8743

Typeset by DOCUPRO, Sydney
Printed by Southwood Press, Sydney

10 9 8 7 6 5 4 3 2 1

Contents

For the mothers and the sons who took part . . .

For my son, Josh
and for Graham, who was Lotte's son.

Preface

Until I wrote this book, I had no idea how little I knew about masculinity. My ignorance was not unique. It was typical. I was the 'typical' mother of a son. More than anything else, writing this book has taught me how fundamental it is that women who mother boys develop a realistic understanding of the socialisation process which creates what is called 'masculinity'. It has made me realise that it is a woman's ignorance of 'masculinity' that is her downfall in the relationship with her boys. We blunder through lack of knowledge.

My own son had no direct involvement in this book. I did not either discuss it with him or question him about the topics the book explores but, just being his mother has taught me a lot. The fact that I have experience as the 'mother of a son' informs the whole work. Two personal observations were particularly significant in making me think generally about the relationship and they would not have occurred if I had had no male child. First, watching the playground socialisation at his primary school, I realised that fundamentally, girls pair but boys group. Misled by a female perspective, I had been waiting, as had other mothers, to meet my son's first 'best friend'. The second incident was not an isolated one, but a recurring trend. Time and again, I saw mothers being told what to do, where to go and indeed, where to get off by their young sons. I watched the women accept it. At first I thought that contemporary mothers were failing feminism. Instead, I have discovered that feminism has failed the mothers of sons.

It is fashionable to interpret women as being victims of male culture and, often, they are. But that is not the whole story. I make no apologies for calling on my own sex to recognise that they need more knowledge about masculinity. It is because I shared that female ignorance that I feel entitled to make such a demand. And because the mothers who contributed to this book confirmed my belief that women have the courage to seek understanding whatever the pain to themselves.

As a feminist woman, I have faith in the modern female viewpoint. On most subjects, it is acute and empathetic. Despite these general gains, I found much evidence that, in relation to sons, it is too often blinkered by romantic or psychological stereotypes about males. Feminism, in this respect, has been counterproductive. The mother–son relationship has altered in recent years—and for the better—but it is not a contradiction to claim that it is also curiously old-fashioned. Quarantined from feminist influence, its dynamics have survived substantially intact during the same decades which have wrought much change for daughters.

I decided to write the book because I felt that there was a disjunction in the way contemporary boys and girls were raised and the possibility that the changes wrought by feminism might perpetuate the gap between the sexes rather than bridge them, dismayed me. I did not understand what I was taking on. Initially, I made the classic error of expecting to write about women and from the female point of view. The most salutary discovery of all was the light shed by men's opinion about the relationship with their mothers and the discrepancy it revealed between male and female perspectives. And it posed the question: does this same discrepancy exist today?

This work suggests some answers. I am not a psychologist of either the professional or the 'pop' variety. It will be for the former to explore the questions raised in more depth. My aim was to analyse the relationship to a level beyond my personal opinion and to highlight the common patterns of experience and feelings. The comparison between past and present patterns was designed to clarify the subject further.

My research is attitudinal and anecdotal. It reflects the opinions and the feelings of mothers and sons over the generations from post World War II to the 1990s. I accumulated material and then allowed the material itself to lead me to my conclusions—I had followed this method previously when researching *A Cargo of Women*. I read widely to substantiate as much of the research as possible but I found little material of direct relevance. The reading did provide useful background, however, and it also sharpened my perceptions when dealing with the primary material.

The mothers and sons who took part were drawn from Australia and Great Britain in the approximate ratio of 60:40 (many Australian-based participants had spent their youth in Britain). The Australian contribution however included, directly or indirectly, a significant number of other nationalities, particularly Yugoslav,

Dutch, German, Polish, Chinese and, to a lesser extent, Italian and Greek. It is fair to say that the sample was mainly Western, Anglo-Saxon/Celtic and predominantly middle-class.

One hundred and fifty-three adult women took part, their ages ranging from 23–83 years but with most clustered between 33–70 years of age. The female view was expanded further by the contribution of 54 teenage girls aged between 12–15 years. There were contributions from 129 men and boys whose ages ranged from 10–72 years. These were mainly divided into two groups, one from 38–54 years and another from 13–27 years. Contributions were obtained by a mixture of direct interview, written response to questionnaires and vocal response using a self-administered tape recorder. Some mothers and sons were pairs. Most were not. Participants were sought at random through appeals on radio, in magazines and newspapers and, in Australia, also from newsletters of the Nursing Mothers' Association and the NSW Hospital Auxiliaries.

The nature and scope of the book and the fundamental approach of following where the material led me meant that twice its pivot changed substantially. The first came with the realisation that the male point of view needed to be expressed; the second centred around the emphasis in the material on the detrimental role not of some abstract concept about 'male culture' but of the personal, intimate impact of masculine socialisation and women's ignorance of its processes. I expected men to lack self-awareness on the subject; women's misconceptions caught me by surprise.

The contributions from men equalled the women for courage and honesty in articulating their feelings about a relationship of great importance to them. These contributions revealed the obvious isolation of most of the men and their utter lack of knowledge that the feelings expressed were part of a widely shared pattern. One of my hopes for the book is that it might become a conduit for information between men; that by reading it, a man might discover that he is not alone with his uncertainty or ambivalence and that his mixed feelings about his mother are neither his inadequacy—nor hers.

The young men and boys also approached the task with a frankness that made me respect as well as like them. But I was dismayed by the commonality with their fathers' generation when one said to me: 'I'm keen to do it. There's nowhere else we can talk about it'.

A combination of the project's intrinsic difficulty and a personal crisis caused me to lose confidence half-way. I was picked up and dusted down by my friend Sherri Stumm who lent me her energy and enthusiasm until I regained my own. It is hard to express my gratitude sufficiently except to say that this book is hers also. My regular support squad never faltered either although I leaned heavily on them. Friends Penny Nelson, Rhonwen Cuningham, Tom Breen and Prue and Michael Lindsay helped me enormously. So did my brother and sister-in-law Robert and Janine Macfarlan who lent me their beach house where I thumped out the final chapters in solitude. Jan Fitzhardinge, Christina Mowbray-Jaffrey, Sharon Mitchell and Thelma Ferris each made a major contribution. Many other people combined forbearance and encouragement towards a friend who veered from abstraction to absence. The latter includes Norma Townsend to whom I owe special thanks for sharing Virgil. I made several long-distance friends and now look forward to personal meetings with Marion Andrews, Geraldine Taylor and June and David de Vaus. My gratitude is extended particularly to Portia Barnes, Ita Buttrose, who gave me much help through her magazine, ABC broadcaster, Rachael Kohn and Geraldine Doogue who also helped while compering *Offspring* on ABC radio. There were others who helped but cannot be named for reasons of privacy. I cannot emphasise enough how I valued their contribution.

Writing the book has been a personal voyage of discovery fuelled by that strongest of motives: the personal—my own son's future—and the political—my profound support for the women's movement and the belief that it has opened up a pathway to more fulfilling relationships both for, and between, the sexes. But I shared this journey every step of the way with the mothers and sons who came with me and for whom I developed much affectionate respect. Their voices can be heard throughout the text. The dedication of the book reflects my appreciation to them and, as always, to my husband and son for bearing with me so supportively.

Babette Smith
Sydney, 1994

1 The masculine framework

The 'male culture' has traditionally defined mothers as being 'the problem' in boys' lives. Western culture abounds with the theme of sons 'coping' with their mothers, 'escaping' from them, or rejecting them in order to be a 'real' man. Inconceivably in a feminist era, women still internalise these images and allow them to dictate the way in which they behave with their sons. Women doubt their own judgment. Their sense of entitlement is slight. But women are not the only ones to suffer in this relationship. Men damage themselves by complying with an idea of masculinity which is so narrow that, unknowingly, they become victims as well. It is not possible to analyse the mother–son relationship without stumbling over the destructive influence of the male culture but it will not be possible to change it without taking account of the masculine perspective.

For centuries, women have mothered male children without understanding the masculine culture of which their boys are part. Most are unaware of their ignorance and men do not comprehend its effect so neither sex ever discusses the subject. Women, as mothers, are usually just blamed for the repercussions of their lack of knowledge while the nature of their misunderstanding remains hidden, even from themselves.

Mothers do not understand masculinity for a number of reasons. The most obvious and fundamental is that the boy child is indeed the 'opposite sex'. Adopting another's perspective is always difficult and it would be foolish to argue that this intriguing difference can be abolished into a shared androgynous understanding. The biological difference will not change, nor will the contrary point of view which results. It is the exaggerated versions of this difference—the cultural codes of behaviour and attitudes which Western society designates as appropriate femininity and masculinity—which need to be challenged.

The struggle to understand the differences between male and female is complicated by dense layers of cultural and religious meaning built up and solidified over centuries. The fundamental purposes of the two sexes—a female designed to reproduce and nurture the species and a male whose role was to procreate and defend it—still exist beneath the encrustation of the past. These gender-specific features have become increasingly inappropriate and uncomfortable for both men and women. Feminism as a movement aimed to redress the imbalance which had developed in the female role and, to some extent, it is succeeding. Male role conditioning in the Western world, however, has remained essentially unchanged from the form it has taken for millennia, even though it is increasingly exposed as being unsuitable for its contemporary environment.

Past emphasis on separately defined roles for both sexes and, more recently, the lingering, pervasive assumptions about them, have acted as a barrier to women's knowledge of a man's world. They allowed romance to flourish at the expense of reality, encouraging women to cherish and perpetuate romantic stereotypes which structure the relations between masculine and feminine, oblivious to the way in which these obscure the actuality of being male. Misled by romance, they prefer to idealise the difference between femininity and masculinity rather than seeking to understand it. In adult relationships, this sentimental blindness can be an enjoyable matter of choice, but when similar distortions are extended to children, it has repercussions on women's mothering of boys. The gathering impact of 'masculinity' on the child is masked by the stereotype, just as assumptions about femininity once concealed its ill-effects on girls. Diverted by the notion of a 'young man' and presuming the existence of innate masculine characteristics, some mothers do not distinguish between the fully-realised masculinity of an adult male and the emotional needs of a growing boy. They miss the imposition of masculine culture and the way it changes their boys from without, obstructing rather than enhancing what was originally within.

A further obstacle to women's understanding of the nature of masculinity has been their subordinate position in a male dominated society. Women could not fully appraise masculine culture while they were excluded from experiencing it. Nor could they develop the capacity to conceptualise it while their inferior status meant they lacked education. Feelings of inadequacy, in their own minds as well as others, devalued their judgments to 'just' personal opinion. As long as women were restricted to the home environment, their human interaction limited to domestic affairs and their intellectual development circumscribed by ideas about female inferiority and the supremacy of 'female instinct', the need for those who were mothers of sons to understand developing masculinity was not apparent. Nor did it seem relevant so long as women complied with men's definition of the meaning of 'female'. Derek Llewellyn Jones, author of *Everyman* pointed out that adopting the perspective of the powerful is a well-documented defence tactic. By this means, women could avoid the anxiety of perceiving their own oppression. It also maintained the status quo. 'Anthropologists have found that many represssed minority groups tend to adopt the attitudes of the stronger dominant group towards themselves. Women may do the same by accepting the submissive stereotype . . .'[1]

One modern mother who contributed to this study was frustrated by her experience with women who accepted the feminine stereotype. Recognising that it would not be combatted on an individual basis for her son's generation, she pinned her hope on the greater feminisation of the society in which he lived.

> *I have seen many mothers of my age (fifty) letting their sons dominate them. I've spoken to them about it. They sincerely associate love with physical slavery for the males in their lives and claim this is the only way they can show their love. I think 'male chauvinists' must have been unwittingly encouraged by their mothers. To enhance her own self-esteem, a mother liked to think that the male couldn't do the domestic things as well as she could. She had been denied the chance to be as well-educated as her husband and he enjoyed putting down her intellectual ability. She felt completely inferior and she 'acted' stupid. It hasn't changed. I worked with a committee of women at a boys' school. They were talented and hard working. Their combined strength was quite powerful. They could all have been chairmen of BHP if they had the training, but they hadn't even the confidence to propose a vote of thanks at a meeting. So this was the average 'mother' for the present generation of males aged 20–30. At least, because they have females studying and working alongside them, the young men are sensitive and try to understand a woman's point of view in a way rarely seen in our generation of men. Surely a young man with*

these qualities will have an enriched life? That is how I see it for my son.

A consequence of accepting the male definition of 'femininity' has been that women acceded to men's version of 'masculinity'. Indeed, they believe, and collude in, the myths, legends and noble motives which disguise the unpalatable reality of masculine culture. The ornamental version presents heroes rather than warmongers, competition rather than aggression, wisdom rather than power, love rather than possession, chivalry not supremacy. It claims to be logical instead of unfeeling, asserts independence and not dependence, mastery never uncertainty. Through the centuries, women have supported the rationale that greater purposes, beyond their comprehension, informed masculine rituals, justifying any characteristics that they might find distressing to their feminine natures. Men know the hard truth about masculinity, but dare not articulate it for fear of being called unmanly. Women have long been deceived by the embellishments. Together the sexes have propped up the romantic superstructure, but even today, women's lack of perspective blinds them to the reality behind the facade. When the veil occasionally lifts, they decide that what they glimpse is the exception not the rule of men's conditioning.

Women's submission to this male definition has had special implications for mothers of boys. It requires them to concede ignorance of matters masculine and defer to the better judgment of men. Colluding in their own rejection, they traditionally obeyed the dictates of male legend, dutifully handing over their male children for rearing by the fathers. And such primitive practices are still fundamental to Western society's expectations. They have been identified, codified and legitimised by anthropologists and harnessed to religion, social and cultural systems and to the ubiquitous Freudian theory and its heirs and offshoots. In recent years Robert Bly, modern interpreter of the myth-laden process of becoming a man, reinforced the enduring influence of these tales in his bestselling book *Iron John.* Bly emphasised their longevity and widespread practice as justification for perpetuating them:

> . . . most cultures describe the first stage of initiation as a sharp and clean break with the mother . . . When 'gender issues', as we

> call them, are well understood, the women do not oppose the initiatory work with the boys, nor helplessly yearn for it but participate enthusiastically and sadly in the drama of it. The relevant sentence is the one accepted in New Guinea by men and women of eight or so tribes: 'A boy cannot change into a man without the active intervention of the older men'. A girl changes into a woman on her own, with the bodily developments marking the change; old women tell her stories and chants, and do celebrations. But with the boys, no old men, no change.[2]

Author and feminist sympathiser, John Stoltenberg, forcefully challenged such long-accepted wisdom.

> Who are the fathers and the sons who can only be reconciled in sharing disdain for the life of the mother? And who are the sons who have become fathers to turn sons against mothers again and again? This servitude must cease. This inheritance must be refused. This system of owning must be destroyed.[3]

Bamboozled by patriarchal mysticism however, women have complied 'enthusiastically and sadly' for centuries. If they were unhappy with the effect of masculine induction on their sons, they accepted that it was their judgment which was impaired, not the cultural yardstick. With insufficient power to either object to or change an entrenched tradition, their usual response to the impassable 'mystery' of masculinity has been to abrogate understanding. In modern terms this is usually expressed by reactions which range from a despairing 'don't know what gets into them', to an admiring 'boys will be boys'.

Women's acceptance of male judgment at a personal level has predisposed them to accept, or at least not question, male expertise in general. Popular assumptions about the development of male identity have been dominated in the twentieth century by the theories of Sigmund Freud. Freud, too, drew on ancient myths to illustrate his contention that the pivot of male identity was the son's sexual desire for the mother which he must abandon, during what Freud termed the 'Oedipal phase', to identify with his father from fear of the older man's hostility. Certainly Freud provided a magnificent rationalisation of men's aggression towards one another: blame the woman; and created a ready scapegoat for anything that went wrong: blame the mother—perhaps she did not let go or was too seductive or too castrating. Freud gave little weight to interaction between males, particularly the striving for supremacy among the physically stronger sex and the inadequacy created in those who lost their contests. In contrast to Freud, Alfred Adler downplayed the role of sexual desire and emphasised the effect of compensating for perceived inferiorities by striving for power, elements which quickly appear fundamental to any researcher investigating males. Adler's 'inferiority complex' entered popular wisdom, but Freud's theories shaped relationships more widely and more insidiously. However, the theories of possible causes are not the concern of this study. It is the result—how male conditioning shapes male identity and the implications for mothers and sons—which is of interest.

The male culture and its requirements were beyond popular dispute until feminism challenged the received wisdom. In analysing what constituted the traditional female role, women began to see through the facades of masculinity. They began to question whether its attributes were any more innate than the ultra-submissive, subordinate, biologically-constricted qualities designated as exclusively feminine. Was 'masculinity' in its accepted form as much an exaggeration as traditional 'femininity'? By examining 'female' and 'femininity', the women's movement put 'male' and 'masculinity' on the agenda for debate.

In the twenty-five years which have elapsed since modern feminists opened up sex and gender for discussion, experience has taught women that masculinity is not as they had been led to believe. Conditioned, for instance, to accept that rationality and logic were innate male characteristics, women were affronted when neither were displayed in men's defensive, threatened reaction to the demonstrable logic of women's case for equality. Women's misjudgment about how men would react and the subsequent female disillusion, lies at the heart of much bitter altercation between the sexes over two decades. It is only one example of many where women's ignorance of masculinity has been to their detriment.

Andrew Tolson was one of the few men who addressed the

questions which feminism raised about masculinity. As early as 1977, exploring what he termed 'The Limits of Masculinity', he concluded that traditional male–female division of labour meant that masculinity originated in *ambivalence.* The exclusively breadwinning role of the father outside the home was the primary cause of a boy's uncertain masculinity. Without an evident model who was present for him to copy, a boy had to posture and pretend, or continuously struggle for recognition and rewards. As Tolson explained it:

> To the boy, masculinity is both mysterious and attractive (in its promise of a world of work and power) and yet, at the same time, threatening (in its strangeness and emotional distance) . . . It works both ways; attracts and repels in dynamic contradiction. This simultaneous distance and attraction is internalized as a permanent emotional tension that the individual must, in some way, strive to overcome. Self-realization can only be achieved through a confrontation with father's absence; and, by extension, through the emotional uncertainty a boy feels within himself.[4]

Tolson also pointed out that father absence leaves a vacuum for women to 'construct' a boy's idea of masculinity. The mother is left to occupy a pivotal role in interpreting the father (and masculinity in general) to the son. Her interpretation will colour the boy's vision of what is masculine and her view may range anywhere from denigration to idealisation of the father figure and the male world. Some mothers present their sons with an image of masculinity which focuses on family history including their own fathers and grandfathers. Others concentrate on their version of the internal qualities which make 'a good man'. Tolson's theories took account of class variations. He pointed out that middle-class masculinity was based on a vision of personal achievement compared to the more aggressive domestic authoritarianism of working-class masculinity which a boy experienced directly in the home. The childhood of one of the middle-aged contributors to this book illustrated Tolson's opinion in almost every respect. Describing his father as 'remote, strict and authoritarian', he said the older man made him believe he should be 'tough, successful and not make waves', but he always felt that he failed to meet these expectations.

In his father's absence, the boy's mother's views of masculinity prevailed.

> *He was a self-made man and I think he regarded me as being a bit soft. At the same time, if I was being what I considered successful, like playing for the school in the first or second XV, he very seldom came to watch. He was always too tired, or too busy. He wasn't really around . . . I acquired my ideas of what it was to be a man absolutely from my mother. She set the role model. She would speak with pride of her family and what they'd done. Like her father, who went to World War I when he was over age, just because he felt it was the right thing. That's what real men did. A sense of duty. A strong sense of duty. A strong sense of giving to others, unselfishness. If you think of yourself, it's selfish. You should never do that—a man doesn't. Being brought up during the war, the role models were obviously the wartime heroes, generals, air force pilots etc. She pointed out a number of times that these were the qualities—a hero, a self-sacrificer, these were the things that real men did. A man wouldn't cry. To be a man you had to be tough and self-sufficient. I can't really remember my father ever talking about that. And I don't think she ever held him up as a role model. If she did, it was in a business sense—success and hard work, but my understanding of masculinity would certainly have come from her and her perceptions at the time. This was not just when I was young, but later on too. Men should be nice, agreeable, polite, unselfish, self-sacrificing, gentlemen. Anything else was looked on with dislike. (age 53)*

The crucial role that mothers can play in 'creating' masculinity has not been addressed by modern feminists in search of equality between the sexes. It was decades before some feminists realised that they, too, must address the question of men's socialisation. By 1992, a few had clarified their view about 'authorised' masculinity and had begun to speak out. Gloria Steinem gave a succinct description of the 'problem' when she endorsed John Stoltenberg's book, *Refusing to be a Man.* The heart of the matter, Steinem said, is 'a social construct called masculinity that makes men shorten their own lives, distance themselves from children, punish women in their headlong effort to be not-woman, and try to defeat each other'.[5]

Feminist research since the 1960s has concentrated on

uncovering the difference between femaleness and feminine role conditioning. Any discussion of maleness and masculinity has generally arisen as a sideline and the implications for men have not been pursued. Distinctions between sex and gender have essentially reached only the converted. Few men, young or old, revealed any awareness of an argument which maintained that sexuality was not dependent on masculine or feminine behaviour. In the male mind, the two are usually inextricable, the only exception being homosexuals who have a compelling reason to question it.

Men strive to prove their sexuality by reaching some absolute masculine standard. The contributions to this book revealed that those who felt they failed to achieve the desired level were internally devastated. Sons of the post-war decades in particular, who could not emulate the 'real' men, or even give a credible show of toughness, were left with an enduring sense of inadequacy. The discomfort caused by the struggle to fit the masculine yardstick was evident in the following description from a man in his late forties. Although he detected no maternal influence in his masculine development, he did reveal elsewhere that his mother had wanted him to take boxing lessons and this was vetoed by his father. Her reasons are unknown. Perhaps she was scared for her frail boy and anxious to help him cope. Perhaps she believed that, contrary to her retiring, passive husband, 'real' men should be strong and dominant.

> *My mother probably played little part in my understanding of masculinity. My heroes in my younger days were all physically tough, not only tough, they had redeeming qualities as well, but physical and mental toughness were certainly an essential part of their make-up and this is not something that is relevant to Mum. We are not a physically or mentally tough family. One of my favourite books when I was younger was* Somebody Up There Likes Me *by Rocky Graziano, a New York streetfighter, who was for a short time middleweight boxing champion of the world. I remember envying him his hammer-like right hand, and wishing I could punch like that. Probably as a compensation for my basic timidity, I practised judo and karate for a while, and did some weight-training, but I was physically and psychologically totally unsuited to combat sports . . . I'm sure that I have an immature*

and unreliable view of masculinity, and that true masculinity has no element of Rambo in it, but I think I always regarded Mum as being so unable to handle any real conflict situation that I would have discounted anything she told me about behaviour under pressure. I don't think that my parents were very reliable guides toward mature masculinity. (age 47)

Fortunately, there is now much in Western culture which dilutes the more rigid forms of masculinity which prevailed when this man was a child. The male role has widened to include things that were previously condemned as unmanly. But men who have opened up their role—and their thinking—are, with some honourable exceptions, few and far between. Over the age of thirty-five years they are rare as too many have either retreated or 'dug in' stubbornly against what they perceive as an attack rather than an appeal—a reaction which becomes less a matter of resentment and more one of sorrow to women who have grasped that defensiveness is the real basis of masculinity. The truth is revealed in that well-known military adage: 'The best form of defence is attack'. Men fight wars in the same way that they learn to survive their lives.

Nearly twenty years ago, Andrew Tolson pointed out that the road to proper manliness is constantly monitored, but the destination is never doubted. For their own benefit, and for the sake of the people who love them, men need to query the goal. It is unnecessary to put up with the discomfort of the masculine stereotype; if they feel inadequately masculine, they should not judge themselves failures. The question to ask is not, 'What's wrong with me?', but rather, 'What's wrong with masculinity?'.

Consideration of masculinity has become increasingly subtle and profound. In 1986, a Swedish group investigating 'The Changing Role of the Male' concluded:

> It is not merely a question of the need of the child for a father, it also involves the need of men for their children. Men do not necessarily need to be perpetually *on their guard* with their children; they need opportunities to develop and show several sides of their character . . . by preserving a close and daily contact with his children, a man will find scope for enriching his own life.[6] [emphasis added]

Three years after the Swedish study and fifteen years after Andrew Tolson's book was published, John Stoltenberg examined the possibility of refusing to be a 'typical' man. He concluded that the precise construct of masculinity and the pressure to conform to it makes it impervious to criticism. In personal terms, masculinity is a barrier to self-awareness. Stoltenberg claimed that a fundamental reason is the emphasis on the process to the exclusion of the goal. Only one aspect of manhood is ever subject to examination—how a boy develops into a man. Should he play football, go to boarding school, into the army? Is he showing signs of manliness or is he becoming a 'sissie' or, in today's terminology, a wuss? What exactly constitutes 'manhood' and whether or not it is worth achieving, is not questioned. Yet, according to Stoltenberg, it is the very requirements of male identity that result in its core component which he terms 'the evasion of ethical accountability'. Another description is 'lack of empathy'.

> Male sexual identity exists, in part, because people born with penises learn an ethic of sexual injustice, an ethic that leaves out specific others. In order to distinguish themselves as real 'men', they learn not to know what can be known about the values in what they do to others, specifically anyone who is 'less a man' . . . A real man doesn't have to pay attention to the consequences of his act.[7]

In other words, according *to* a man, it is striving to *be* a man which develops disregard in women's sons.

Many women believe that the inability to express feelings is an innately masculine trait but, according to Jerome Kagan, Professor of Human Development at Harvard University, it is a product of Western notions of masculinity. According *to* a man, *becoming* a man, in the Western style, blocks the expression of feelings:

> . . . women in the West are more empathic than men, but this sex difference is not universal. Japanese men are very empathic. It is a tradition in Western society that men achieve and be autonomous and individualistic; women should be nurturing, protective and healing. One can't be achieving, individualistic, and competitive if one is sorry for the victim. Western men must suppress empathy

> for their rivals or fail to accomplish their goals . . . Causing pain is the hardest thing for a woman to do. It is easier for men.[8]

The effects of orthodox masculinity are very much a matter of debate. The discussion has only just begun but even a glimmer of its fundamental nature immediately overturns a vast range of preconceptions, particularly female preconceptions, about men and about boys. It illuminates the struggle that male children must experience to adapt themselves to masculinity. It explains to mothers, the hurtful, bewildering change from affectionate toddlers to remote adults. Boys will be boys not because they were born that way, but because masculinity requires it of them.

2 Post-war mothers

After World War II, the demarcation between male and female roles which had become blurred during wartime returned with exaggerated emphasis. Ideas about 'proper' masculinity and femininity were expressed so clearly and so frequently that men and women, boys and girls, could not fail to absorb them. Both sexes tried to live up to the requirements. Mothers' goal was to prepare their children appropriately to take their place in society but the gulf between the lives of men and women increased maternal ignorance of masculinity. It also placed enormous pressure on boys to meet the community's masculine standard.

The memory of war shaped the way in which women related to their sons during the subsequent years. Male children had always been valued as breadwinners but, in the post-war climate, their status was enhanced by the aftermath of anxiety for their lives. Boys were treasured. Onlookers assumed them to be the objects of their mothers' delight, even to be their mothers' heroes. Sometimes, they were. In Western nations, this delightful idea was reinforced by the all-encompassing ethos of the Judaeo–Christian religion which formed the basis for community assumptions about the importance of the boy's adult role. At every turn, the pervading social climate extolled men as special human beings. The mother of a son was envied and praised just for giving birth to a boy. His arrival conferred prestige on her.

The popular view of the mother–son relationship at this time, however, also contained negative elements. One of the most influential was propagated by American author Phillip Wylie's infamous book, *A Generation of Vipers*.[9] Wylie coined the term 'momism' to describe his archetype of a dominant, all-devouring mother who emasculated her son by her demands and the guilt she laid on him. Other nations tended to regard Wylie's 'moms' as a distinctly American version of motherhood which did not really apply to their own.[10] Nevertheless, the derogatory impact of 'momism' was international. Women of all ages and many countries absorbed the tag as a general warning about how not to behave to their sons. In two generations of female minds (daughters and mothers) it established the *mother* as potentially damaging to her male child.

A Generation of Vipers was originally published in 1942. It was re-issued in the mid-1950s. Wylie has sometimes been accused of triggering the rash of mother-blaming that was prevalent during the 1940s and 1950s, but he was not alone in castigating mothers during that period. 'Mother' as 'culprit' cropped up everywhere, from the media to psychiatric journals. Much of the theorising sprang from the ideas of Sigmund Freud. Author Betty Friedan described the United States at this time as being permeated by a 'Freudian mania'.[11]

Freud's theories burst the confines of professional and academic enclaves to be widely propagated in the mass media. Most mothers—and their growing daughters—absorbed the details of the female role in his famous Oedipus complex: that a son must identify with his father in order to become a man and part of such identification involved rejecting his mother and all things female. A mother's responsibility was to facilitate the rejection of herself or risk endangering her son's masculinity, the greatest hurdle to which, according to the Oedipus theory, was the risk that a mother's sexuality would activate a son's desire for her.

It is unlikely that more than a tiny percentage of mothers had any real knowledge of Freud's theory about the erotic interplay between them and their sons. They were probably conscious only of a vague prohibition against displaying too much physical affection for their boys, an idea prompted by something read in a popular women's magazine, or a warning fleetingly heard from a child-raising expert on the radio. But it was a powerful suggestion and deeply planted. As feminist Adrienne Rich pointed out as late as the mid-1970s:

> Women who have never read Freud are raising their sons in the belief that to show them physical affection is to be 'seductive', that to influence their sons against forms of masculine behaviour they as women abhor is to 'castrate' them or to become the 'devouring', 'domineering' creature that their sons will have to reject in order to grow up mentally 'healthy', or that they, and they alone, are responsible if their sons become 'unnecessarily (sic) homosexual.[12]

Friedan summarised the general result of the 'Freudian microscope' for mothers with sarcastic outrage:

> It was suddenly discovered that the mother could be blamed for almost everything. In every case history of a troubled child; alcoholic, suicidal, schizophrenic, psychopathic, neurotic adult; impotent, homosexual male; frigid, promiscuous female; ulcerous, asthmatic and otherwise disturbed American, could be found a mother. A frustrated, repressed, disturbed, martyred, never satisfied, unhappy woman. A demanding, nagging, shrewish wife. A rejecting, overprotecting, dominating mother. The Second World War revealed that millions of American men were psychologically incapable of facing the shock of war, of facing life away from their 'moms'. Clearly something was wrong with American woman.[13]

Some of the most significant and most quoted examples of the problems resulting from 'bad' mothering were associated with soldiers during World War II but, even if the child's gender was not specified, the mother referred to in these endless Freudian case studies, the widespread media articles and the pronouncements of 'experts', was almost invariably the mother of a son. Yet, at the same time as women with male children absorbed these strictures and fears into their mothering, they strove to comply with the equally strident social dictates that motherhood should be their sole and complete life's work, the source of every satisfaction.

The way in which the war shaped female attitudes to boys was apparent in the comments from women of this generation. Those who experienced the strain and the dread, whether as mother or daughter, mentioned the war as a reason for particularly cherishing males. Their reminiscences were shot through with references to war. And fear of war.

> *In my early teens, my young friends went to war and I didn't see a lot of them again, so I was very afraid when I had my sons.*

> *We were brought up to reverence young men—hadn't they fought and died for us? Might it also be the fate of our sons? Indeed, one of mine was on the list for Vietnam when thankfully that war ended.*

A grandmother in her sixties recalled the practical effect of war on the relationship between a mother and her boys and its consequences for maternal behaviour.

> *Two world wars greatly influenced the way mothers brought up their*

sons. My mother-in-law had lost her husband in World War I. She relied very heavily on the three older boys. Then her eldest son went to World War II. She needed her next two boys to take over the father role and to do a man's work on the farm. It's not easy to send your fifteen-year-old son out to cut 40 ton of wood a year, as well as milk, plough and harvest. Of course, she waited on them, hand and foot. They were her substitute husband, keeping her in a job, feeding her five younger children and providing them all with a home.

Domesticity received an enormous impetus from the return of the surviving servicemen. The popular image of the 1950s is predominantly a family one—husband, wife and children, any number of children, but usually more than two. Families of three, four and five children were common. An only child was the object of pity. Wives carried out their child-rearing in a social climate which heavily promoted motherhood as a career. It was also regarded as the only true fulfilment for women and society looked askance at any alternative female occupation. In general, women themselves did not question this view. Most tried hard to live up to the highest ideals of motherhood—to be unselfish and put others' needs first, to be always available, to love and to nurture.

The high regard for motherhood stemmed from more than a simple belief that it was the ultimate feminine vocation. It included also the concept of women as 'God's police'. Mothers were seen as responsible for imparting specific religious as well as general moral values. Their status was enhanced by this respectful community view, but the pressure to conform could also be heavy.

Religion caused me great grief in rearing my children. I copped it on all sides. I was Anglican, my husband Roman Catholic. The priests told me that I wasn't really married because I didn't change my religion, although eventually I sent all my children to Catholic schools. My own friends turned against me. I had it on both sides. (age 69)

The emphasis on religious or moral training varied from mother to mother, but the post-war era undoubtedly continued the traditional expectation that mothers were the guardians of these values.

Women were judged by the standard of their mothering. If children's behaviour, manners, dress, cleanliness, sometimes even health, were less than perfect, it was mothers who were held accountable. They could be censured by the wider community through the medium of church, school or social groups or, at a personal level, by critical relatives. Husbands, too, were often quick to criticise. Dirty children or naughty children were their mothers' failure.

For these reasons, and also out of loving pride, most mothers cared a great deal about how their children looked and how they behaved. Children of both sexes had little idea of the kind of pressure which could be brought to bear on their mothers, nor did they appreciate the women's proud wish to show them off. Wriggling in resentful discomfort, as children have always done, they did not understand the fuss.

> *My son surprised me recently by asking, 'What kind of mother were you?'—for insisting always on good manners, to speak correctly, no bad language. Also, I made all their clothes when they were very young, used mainly linen, then always starched their trousers, etc. My son felt that was for my benefit, so people would say 'What nicely dressed children', 'How well-mannered they are' etc. (age 69)*

In this social context, motherhood could resemble an endless public and private test, which women were obliged to pass. At a time when most mothers had several children, it could also be a sentence to very hard labour. Despite a shortage of servants in the United Kingdom after the war, a tradition of 'char ladies' meant middle-class mothers had some help. In countries such as Canada or Australia, newly-arrived European migrants were a limited source of domestic help. Generally, human assistance was scarce and technology had barely begun to mass-produce labour-saving devices for housewives. Most women, including many who were financially comfortable, did all the chores themselves. A doctor's wife, aged sixty-two, reported:

> *I didn't have a car, or mod. cons. Washing dishes was hard work because a kettle had to be boiled . . . It would take all morning to do the washing—boiling the copper, then sloshing the clothes into the tubs and from there into a water-driven spin dryer attached to the tubs. What joy when we could buy a Hoover handwringer machine in 1959. Then sheer heaven when, eventually, I was able to 'dial and disappear'.*

The clear and unequivocal division of roles affected the women's own behaviour and also the way they prepared their sons for manhood. The demarcation was particularly apparent around the house: husbands worked outdoors while inside the house was the wives' responsibility. Most men did not feel any obligation to help with 'women's work'. Those who did were regarded as being very 'good' husbands indeed. But the demarcation existed most immutably between the adults. In some households there was little or no difference concerning children of either sex. With a vast number of tasks and no help, either human or technological, many mothers perpetuated a long tradition by recruiting their children into service. Without the assistance of their sons and daughters, few women could have coped with the large families and sheer volume of work which had to be done. Regardless of sex, they marshalled their often mutinous troops in the manner of a sergeant-major. In doing so, they assumed their children saw the logic of their actions and understood.

> *In the 1940s and 1950s, women had to run the home, do washing, ironing, cooking, bath children and every possible chore that was considered to be a woman's job. I dedicated my life to it at the time. Later, I made my sons and daughters share the workload, whether it was the dishes, polishing floors, making beds. My sons often rebelled, so did the girls, against the strict routine, but the more they did, the bigger their reward. Their help gave me more time to make the girls a new frock, or go and watch the boys play sport.*

Getting the work done, raising 'obedient' and 'well-mannered' children, enforcing the rules and regulations of the home, inculcating moral and ethical values, all fell on a mother's shoulders. It was part of the maternal 'job description' to uphold these standards. Pragmatically, this meant that most women took responsibility as front-line disciplinarians. Strict, often physical, discipline was the prevailing philosophy. 'Giving in' was a sign of weakness. It required constant and rigid enforcement to approach the standards assumed to be necessary. Mothers coped as best they could, with varying degrees of success. Some found it too hard and took thankful refuge in submissive femininity, or rationalised that their role should be to compensate for their husbands' tough stand.

I enjoyed their childhood, I suppose because I didn't need to enforce any strict rules because their father made very strict guidelines which we all adhered to. (age 71)

Fathers' role varied from being used as a threat to administering a beating, which was the ultimate punishment. Such was a father's authority however, that often a stern instruction was sufficient to extract compliance with a mother's wishes.

He left the children's upbringing to me, saying that as I was doing a good job, he saw no reason to interfere. However, the few times he thought any of them were over-stepping the mark, he was quick to say, 'Do as your mother asks'. (age 70)

Women believed that boys were taught to respect them by such paternal instructions.

Male children of this era usually experienced their mothers as very powerful and, in the small details of daily life, they often were. Their boys felt the harassment to get things done and what they described as 'meddling', but most could neither see their mothers' underlying inability to assert themselves nor the limited context of their authority. Several men recounted bitterly how their mothers drilled them in domestic chores while casting muttered aspersions against 'useless men'. They did not realise that they were the recipients of oblique criticisms of their fathers by women whose personal lack of self-esteem made them incapable of voicing their complaints directly. Resenting their husbands, who relaxed around the house while they continued to work, they had resolved to raise their sons differently.

A woman's supremacy in rearing the children and her power as a disciplinarian were often little more than an illusion. Behind most mothers was a father's authority. Generally, wives as well as children were expected to obey their husbands. A man's attitudes and needs were the pivot around which the household revolved. Many sons were fooled into thinking that women were powerful because their mothers upheld their fathers' authority in public. Sometimes the women were frightened to disagree but many held the genuine and widely propagated belief that parents should 'maintain a united front'. Their boys did not know that behind closed doors many women fought for their children before finally complying with their husbands' decisions. Some submitted against their better judgment, others became convinced that their husbands were right after all.

> *I was quite happy with the fact that his father disciplined him where necessary and I am sorry now for the times I interfered when I thought he was being too hard. I now realise it was for the good of the boy. (age 72)*

The extent to which male authority could become intimidation was demonstrated by the wives who rushed fearfully to get the meal underway before their husband came home. Some felt obliged to uphold the rules which the head of the house had laid down even if he was absent and it was an emergency.

> *Just when I needed a son to drive me and his younger brothers around, it was not allowed. I stuck to what his father said and drove everyone myself.*

The upshot of this kind of subordination was to disadvantage women in exercising authority over their sons. The boys could see that their fathers' orders held sway even when the men were absent. Consequently, it could be a major struggle to make them heed a female voice and particularly hard for the many women who found exerting their will personally difficult and somehow alien to their nature anyway. Even a self-confident single mother of that era could strike problems.

> *It took more effort to establish the behaviour I expected from the boys and they did give me a harder time before they co-operated.*

Standards of masculinity also made boys reluctant to obey women. During the post-war decades the clearly divided gender roles meant that there were precise ideas of what was deemed appropriate behaviour for boys—letting females tell them what to do was not included. The strictures about masculinity could be another test for mothers. Raising a boy who appeared to be a 'sissie' could incur severe disapproval. It was a mark of a mother's failure and a personal slight to the father. Even outsiders felt free to express their views. 'Some neighbours thought my elder son was a bit too "quiet"'.

Fathers were assumed to be the experts and most men held particularly strong opinions about how their sons should be reared.

> *My husband was very keen on boxing—they had to be made men, stand up for themselves. I disagreed with some of this as it had a very adverse effect on my second son who had a co-ordination problem due to a difficult birth.*

Sole female parents faced a great challenge in a society which divided men and women so completely but, despite the importance of a husband, some women were forced to manage without one. The war left many widows. In addition, mothers had to cope alone when husbands died later of war wounds, or through accidents, or were 'lost' through marital breakdown. A considerable number raised three, four or more boys by themselves. The burden which this imposed on them in a male-dominated culture has never been fully recognised. With no husband to 'make' their boys respect their wishes and with community respect strictly limited to their maternal and domestic role, they lacked authoritative status both inside and outside the home. Even the widows of soldiers were ranked socially by the circumstances of their husbands' death.[14]

Women who were sole parents strained to be both father and mother at a time when the two roles were foreign to each other. Few women had the self-confidence or the training to assert themselves easily about financial or business affairs and although many were the guardians of cultural pursuits such as music or reading, the majority had only minimal education. On most subjects, single women would have felt unable openly to disagree with male advice. They had to find paid jobs when it was widely asserted that working women risked turning their children into juvenile delinquents. In a world based on pairs, many had a very hard and lonely time despite the well-meaning protection of male relatives and friends. The lucky ones found sustaining friendships among other women. One mother, now eighty years of age, recalled:

> *I often wished for support and help in making decisions, for someone to share the responsibility, for a stern male voice when dealing with the boys. Generally speaking, boys are more inclined to heed their fathers, considering their mothers a 'soft touch' . . .*

In the fifties, single mothers could be made to feel not quite 'all there' so you felt even more alone and, at times, an object of pity.

The mothers who raised children during the war and its aftermath are now women in their seventies and eighties. Their reminiscences are predominantly loving, positive and optimistic. Some obviously skated over difficulties, but more in the vein of playing them down rather than intending to conceal. There was no doubt that they loved their sons and had found joy in rearing them. With deep and abiding pleasure they described their boys, recalling their pranks, their habits and their sayings with nostalgic affection. They were curiously reticent about the present.

Few of these mothers directly answered the question about whether they enjoyed their sons' company. Nor did they supply details of what they discussed or what activities they shared as adults. Occasionally, their pursuit of further education or intellectual hobbies were mentioned as something which sons supported with interest and practical advice but generally, there was a noticeable vacuum around the subject of the present relationship between mother and son. The following was exceptional for both its enthusiasm and its detail.

I thoroughly enjoy the relationship with my three sons, each is so different and so special to me. With my eldest son, we talk about his work as a teacher, lots of educational issues as he actually fulfilled my own dream of becoming a teacher, his plans for his home, his future and that of his children. We discuss my ideas of what I'm looking for in retirement, which is imminent. He gives me advice. Sometimes I take it, sometimes not. We both have very definite ideas about what we would like to do. Our politics differ, but from our experience as parents, we know that he will probably change, so make sure it doesn't become an abrasive issue. I always feel it is great to hear his point of view. I wish I had the opportunities in life he has had and, to an extent, I envy him. He is interested in my involvement in the local branch of the Hospital Auxiliary and when I am taking part in an essay competition, he posts me relevant literature and encourages my efforts. (age 69)

This kind of lively detail was unusual. Generally, the women in this age group were so vague that it was impossible to establish with certainty whether they were deliberately skirting the subject or simply regarded their present relationship as somehow irrelevant to their maternal role. In many cases, it appeared that details of common interest were displaced by an interpretation of how their sons behaved to them: 'loving and caring . . . he appreciates me more now'; 'always considerate . . . and respects my opinion'; 'they are considerate to me and their sister and respect our opinions'.

When asked if their relationship with their sons was emotionally rewarding or, perhaps, disappointing, mothers tended to respond with positive generalities. Few expressed any reservations. One notable contribution on this topic came from the eighty-year-old widow who had longed for 'a stern male voice' when dealing with her growing sons. Alone since her children were toddlers, she had worked full-time to support them, experiencing a combination of job and motherhood which linked her to many younger women in the following decades. And there were other similarities. Like so many later female sole parents, her instincts were for a democratic family style and she developed an increasingly egalitarian companionship with her sons and daughter during their adolescence. This approach would be duplicated later by many female-led families, but its democratic style was rare for that period.

> *. . . as the children grew older, a real sense of companionship developed, helped by my readiness to listen and discuss a wide range of subjects. I talked to them as adults, never talking down. If my husband had lived, I would have discussed problems with him, instead I talked to the children. On one occasion my elder son, then all of fifteen, patted me on the shoulder and said, 'Don't worry, Mum, it will be all right'. In typical male fashion, he did nothing, nor offered any solution! . . . They did not seek my advice as they do now in their forties. As a youngster and in adolescence, my eldest son was never 'chatty' with me like his sister. On the other hand, we did really communicate. Today, he is very self-reliant, making his own decisions, only occasionally asking my advice. My younger son went through a particularly torrid divorce a few years ago. Because of that traumatic time, he and I have a special relationship. We discuss all sorts of issues, politics, religion (beliefs not sects), what do I think about his plans to alter the house, how to landscape the garden and what to plant.*

The descriptions of these now elderly mothers varied in detail according to their circumstances. There were glimpses of the financial hardship and emotional struggles which some had experienced, but virtually all of them confirmed the cultural assumption that the mother–son bond is mutually strong and loving and, undoubtedly, rewarding.

But how accurate was this generation's perception of the relationship with their sons? Doubt was cast by their sons' wives. The younger women told a very different story. Their observations of their husbands' feelings and behaviour towards their mothers were overwhelmingly negative. 'Never on easy terms' was one of the milder comments by comparison with 'non-existent', or 'their relationship is appalling'. Several wives emphasised that their husbands maintained only the minimum contact necessary: 'does what he has to by way of visits, but nothing else'. Even more extreme were the two women whose husbands had not spoken to their mothers for many years, one because he felt that she had betrayed him, although he could not remember how, the other because his mother would not apologise for something she had said.

Most surprising of all was the frequent comment by so many wives that their husband's mother had not shown him love. She was 'too busy to show affection', one man told his wife. And, 'very emotionally cold towards her children' was how a woman described her mother-in-law. 'Did not show affection', reported many. The younger women held the older ones unequivocally responsible for the long-term effects on the men. 'Scarred all her sons by her inability to share her love with them', declared one wife. 'Made them emotional cripples', claimed another.

Even the positive descriptions tended to be qualified.

My husband as a son is caring, but doesn't go out of his way to write or telephone. In emergencies, he would be there.

Only a small percentage of what daughters-in-law said contained the elements which were supposed to be widespread. The following description of a loving son was unusual.

My mother-in-law was a sweetie . . . My husband loved her very dearly, was very protective indeed. She was widowed many years ago and my husband kept in close touch and had back-up plans to ensure she was OK. If she was ill, he would fetch her and we looked after her here.

Women's opinions of their husband's relationship with his mother arose originally as a sideline to questions about their relationships with their *own* son. It almost forced itself forward as a topic in its own right—and a puzzling one. Was this a true account of how older mothers and their now middle-aged sons related to one another? Or was it actually a problem between two women? The answer would only be found in the responses from sons of that era.

Women get little feedback from their male children. Their relationship with their daughters may be any variation from feisty and competitive, resentful and sullen, grudgingly dutiful, or friendly and joyful. Mothers can assess its condition with a fair degree of accuracy because they have the advantage of a common gender to sharpen their perception and because, like themselves, daughters can and do express their emotions. Sons are different. They are harder for mothers to 'read'. The masculine ethos allows boys to keep their intimate feelings to themselves making mothers feel intrusive. Traditionally, women have never questioned their boys' remoteness. They accept they must 'lose' their sons in this way because the nature of true masculinity demands it. Most of this generation had the refrain off pat: men are busy as 'breadwinners'; their careers require them to move away; or the demands of a new family make it impossible to remain emotionally close to their mothers. Women have long consoled themselves with this rationale, accepting it as the hard but nobly self-sacrificing lot of any mother who bears a son. If the suspicion crosses their mind that their male children are remote because they want to be, most suppress it. It takes a deeply unhappy mother to throw off the contented, reassuring mask and give voice to her misgivings.

I am treated with no more kindness, love or respect than the lady over the road. The last time he touched me was eight years ago, on the day of his marriage. You may ask why don't I kiss him? It's hard to kiss a 6'4" face when it won't bend . . . I have a close, loving relationship with my daughter and her grown family and with my daughter-in-law and the young ones, so where did things go wrong? It is so hurtful that, most times, I block it out of my mind as there seems no point in spending my last years crying over something I seem to have no control over . . . To be fair my son shows no affection for anyone apart from his wife and children, but I feel that, maybe, I could be sort of special and I really have tried hard to earn that right. (age 67)

Mothers long to know how their sons really feel. Eagerly, they search for clues. Or for proof. They are blocked from forming a confident judgment by the assumptions of a different gender and by the men's reticence. Perhaps this is why women cling so hard to the idealised concept of mothers and sons. More often than we know, it may be all they have.

3 Post-war sons

The contributions from sons of the 1950s dovetailed with their wives' claims. What they had to say about their mothers was as startling as it was sad. So many gave the lie to the much-heralded relationship. Their descriptions revealed men trying to reconcile deeply ambiguous feelings which, contrary to female assumptions, were not simply generated by the difficulty of remaining 'a man' while loving your mother. These sons were struggling to love where they had little respect, to believe they *were* loved when they remembered no affection, to justify their love by saying their mother was *not typical.* They were trying to process sorrowful resentment, made even worse because they feared it was unusual as well as unacceptable. The relationship fell short of the ideal, but each son felt that he, alone, was the exception to the rule.

A notable source of sons' ambivalence stemmed from Western society's definition of mothers, the 'ideal' which women strain so hard to emulate. In living up to the multifaceted demands to be inculcator of moral values, inspiration and motivator, protector and helper, source of love, comfort and nurturance, mothers are sustained by the fond belief that their children (in this case, boys) understand and appreciate their efforts. Feminist research into daughters' attitudes threw doubt on that consolation by revealing that the girls tend to scorn it as weakness or stupidity.

The reactions of these, now middle-aged men also contradict some of their mothers' most cherished beliefs. Their experience of the traditional maternal role gave most of them little pleasure and much discomfort. At a personal level, the very qualities which are supposedly the hallmark of a 'good' mother were often the subject of criticism. Women believe there is no greater sign of maternal love than dedication to their children yet one son from the middle of a large family described 'total dedication' as 'too much closeness'. In theory, unselfishness is hailed as a noble feature of mothering but, in practice, men did not experience it that way. A son mentioned how he disliked 'the way she doesn't express her own needs'. He softened the criticism by admitting it was difficult for anyone to express needs around his father. Sometimes the sons felt exasperated: 'it can be irritating to have someone who is a continual provider, but not an equal'. In other circumstances, a mother's obvious subordination of her needs made her son feel guilty. 'The worst thing I think was the way she made herself a martyr to what everyone else wanted'. Even men whose mothers avoided burdening them with guilt, were not entirely happy and struggled not to admit actual resentment about their mother's unselfishness.

> *Even though I feel she should have put herself first sometimes, I can't help admiring the persistence and determination she has shown over the years in living for all the members of her family.*

The gender hierarchy of the 1950s with its strict division of male–female roles, prevented most sons from recognising favouritism from their mothers. What to their sisters was blindingly obvious devotion, seemed the natural order of things to the boys. Few men believe that they received special attention, let alone maternal adoration. If asked directly, most will deny being favoured, but the denial springs from lack of insight or the oblivion created by years of entitlement rather than a stubborn refusal to recognise an advantage. And because they were never conscious of it, they felt no benefit. Indeed, the classic, never-wavering mother love could be particularly annoying when they knew anger was warranted. Even a description as fond as the following, contained its careful undertones:

> *She is . . . always giving, never bears grudges for the times when I've hurt her feelings, constantly looks for things to give me, or to do for me. Her love was constant, even when she disapproved.*

Nor did a woman's lack of power or the impact of a dominant husband attract the sympathy that some mothers might have expected. Even if the sons understood the inequality with hindsight, most were oblivious to its implications as children or they wondered—and some still do—why she 'let' him dominate. They resented their fathers' behaviour, but only a few were sufficiently sorry for their mother to become her confidante and ally. The following was an exception:

> *[She] has always believed that her potential was severely restricted, first by her family and, later, within her relationship with my father*

. . . I would like her to be the strong and educated person that she has influenced me to be.

The functions of religious and moral guardian gave mothers status in the community, but it was often a source of conflict, confusion or sorrow to their sons. Most women took this responsibility very seriously and not many had sufficient confidence to wear it lightly and pass it on gently. Some bore it like a cross to be inflicted on their children. Others wore it like a cloak of righteousness. Many were almost certainly intimidated by the responsibility of forcing an often large and unruly brood to obey. Within the narrow conformity of the prevailing social order, their failure could be public and humiliating. Any one of a myriad misdemeanours could attract ready censure: a pregnant daughter; a son caught stealing; not attending Mass; inappropriate dress—a neckline too low, no gloves, no hat for church; a 'slovenly' house. Mothers' response to this community pressure was often a seemingly unreasonable insistence on 'keeping up appearances', an attitude which their sons bitterly resented. One adult man still interpreted his mother's behaviour as:

More concerned with my behaviour and appearance as it appeared to others than consideration for me.

The original religious or moral obligations could be almost obliterated by a strangling class-consciousness which added its own pressure. In some homes, mothers strained to 'do the right thing' in order to avoid being called 'common' but their own fear of the tag did not stop them applying the label to others—almost as though saying it first secured the high ground against similar attack.

Sons remembered this aspect of their mothers with loathing bordering on contempt. Few saw the context sufficiently to feel compassion, most just angrily recalled the effect of such conformity on their childhood, particularly when 'doing the right thing' was mixed up with instructions about sexual behaviour.

She had an obsession with goodness . . . for my brother and me to grow up to be 'good men'. I frequently misunderstood just what she was talking about in her directions and homilies. A boy had to 'behave' himself—till my twenties I assumed that meant a boy shouldn't get drunk, use bad language etc. Her narrowness meant that a good 50 per cent of human experience was suspect, evil, dangerous or 'infra-dig'.

Many sons complained bitterly about their mothers' rigid, dogmatic attitudes. They resented the way the women saw everything in black and white and their stubbornness once they had made up their minds. Their tendency to direct their lives by clinging to small articles of faith drove their sons crazy with irritation, indeed, often physically drove them away.

It is impossible to get mum to objectify her beliefs. She lives all details of her life by little maxims, proverbs like 'waste not, want not'; 'share and share alike'; this makes her unbearable most of the time.

Other men contributed other maternal sayings: 'nothing you ever learn is useless', 'you can have the children, but you don't have to love them', 'behave like a gentleman'.

Pam Peters of the Macquarie University School of Linguistics in Sydney pointed out that individual mothers were not eccentric in acting this way. It was a widespread custom at the time. Peters commented:

We acquire sayings out of the cultural preoccupations of each generation. It's uncertain where many came from . . . Thinking about proverbs and sayings is a 'psychological device' that helps people cope with life.[15]

According to Professor James Tulip, head of Religious Studies at Sydney University, proverbs have a palliative function:

You take a pill and it works for you. It's a perceived truth that's stood the test of time . . . Proverbs are rather like rosary beads, a kind of ritual in words that put you in touch with the wisdom of your culture. They aren't as powerful as they were [in the 1950s]. Our culture today is too active . . . The amateur wisdom of the proverbs doesn't seem to suit the modern professional world.[16]

For the sons of the 1950s, proverbs exemplified characteristics which made them dislike and feel unbearably impatient with their mothers. 'I despised Mum's closed thinking, her inflexibility'. They did not understand that it was often a coping mechanism for unworldly people of little education. The capacity for abstract thought and objectivity is very much a product of education but most mothers of this period left school in their early teens, some even earlier. A son had usually outstripped his mother's formal knowledge by mid-adolescence. Even the minority of women with tertiary education were not encouraged, as females, to explore their intellectual potential. Clever women were a threat. They were also suspected of being unwomanly. Most felt impelled to prove their femininity by abandoning careers or academic achievements and hurrying into marriage.

Social class made little difference, except in style. The same dogmatism and lack of abstract thought was more likely to be expressed in the upper classes as a brittle and frivolous manner. Even women with both the education and time for intellectual depth frequently took the socially acceptable female path of superficiality. Their glossy manners hid the same low self-esteem as their more prosaic working-class sisters. And all shared the preoccupation with class distinctions which women took the lead in delineating and reinforcing[17]—much of their energy was devoted to this end.

Women's experience beyond the home was very limited. Any knowledge they did acquire was usually gained second-hand through their husbands, but the men often saw it as their duty to protect their wives from reality, or assumed that women could not understand anything complicated. Nothing in the women's background, or in their daily lives, enabled them to develop objectivity, broadmindedness, flexibility. It is therefore not surprising that so many sons of this period described their mothers as living by maxims, clinging rigidly to what they knew and believed. Because nothing in their lives prepared them for coping with the unknown or the uncertain, few dared to welcome it and even fewer to seek it. The qualities in mothers which so burden the memories of their adult sons—the slavish nurturing, subordination of self, dogmatic moral principles, determined superficiality, the narrow, subjective, unworldly outlook—reflected the behaviour of women who lacked self-esteem. Incapable of asserting their feelings, they muttered about 'useless men' rather than confronting a man face to face.

They made apple pies, or washed football shorts, rather than saying 'I love you'. They looked sorrowful and manipulated their boys by guilt rather than shouting their anger, or they mocked or admonished sarcastically rather than ordering large adolescent sons from their sight. These were people whose activities and experience were confined to the small territory designated 'female'.

A woman's sphere of influence was precisely defined during this period. Their role was 'homemaker'. In this area they were delegated a great deal of control, which was extended by the simultaneous male divergence into work outside the home. Both parents could be described as the victims of illusion. The emphasis on the authority of men obscured the reality of how women bore most of the daily responsibility for the family, including socialising the children. Their task was made more difficult by their belief in the necessity to raise boys and girls very differently. The result could be a crushing workload.

> With the withdrawal of the father from many areas of family living, a heavy burden is imposed upon the mother and, despite the introduction of numerous labour-saving units, she is probably now working harder and under greater strain than her own mother and grandmother did.[18]

Strain, hard work, uncertainty and insecurity took their toll on many women's personalities. One unusually perceptive son described his mother with vivid insight.

> *A kind of siege mentality, 'conservatism' (not politically), a kind of 'grin and bear it'. I suppose deep emotional rigidity . . . and a physical and emotional stand-offishness and insularity.*

These women had no time to relax. Little opportunity to enjoy. And much worry. Too often, it was necessary to clamp down the emotions of love, or fear, or amusement in order to cope. Only a particularly self-confident woman, or one who was valued and cherished, could flower into the gentle, loving, feminine personality that mothers were supposed to be. Many of their male children looked in vain for the maternal icon and blamed the woman who failed to live up to it.

Psychoanalyst Grete Bibring brought the insights of feminism to bear on these older sons' perceptions. Bibring investigated the effect of 'matriarchal' families, where the mothers were active and strong efficient household managers and generally seemed superior and more competent than their husbands. She summarised the different role of the parents as follows:

> . . . the father did not participate essentially in the upbringing of his children . . . social as well as moral standards, religious and aesthetic values were mostly conveyed by the mother. The same holds true of praise and reprimands. The setting of goals and the supervision of the boy's development lay in her hands. The father appears in all these instances as a friendly onlooker rather than as an important participant.[19]

Such a description fits the situation of many of the sons who took part in this project. They grew up predominantly in their mothers' charge, with their fathers physically absent at work most of the time—in some cases, without fathers at all. Bibring found that sons from her families considered their mothers, as many do here, to be 'rejecting, punitive, ambitious and cold'. (The effect on daughters, incidentally, was quite the opposite. If they came from this type of family, they were more inclined to identify with their mother's active style than they were in families where the mother behaved more passively.) Guided by the sons' descriptions but bringing her female perspective to bear on the women, Grete Bibring concluded that the mothers were, in fact, thoughtful and responsible and that it was the fathers' absence rather than anything the mother actually did that was 'the major factor in determining these attitudes in sons'. In other words, Bibring found a discrepancy between the sons' perceptions and the mothers' actuality. Professor Nancy Chodorow summarised Bibring's findings thus:

> . . . that whatever the social reality and however their mother acted, for these sons, there was simply 'too much mother'.[20]

Too much mother? As a prosaic daily presence, yes, perhaps. Too much organising, harrying, chiding, urging, deciding, reasoning and persuading. Too many unpopular decisions taken. Too many punishments handed out. Too many anxious goals set. Alone.

As the sons of that era matured, they felt it increasingly inappropriate and irksome for a woman to have so much control over them. Often their mothers agreed. Some women backed off completely; others misjudged and continued tactics which had worked when their boys were ten years old. Many settled for a role confined to providing and servicing. And some, with other children still to rear, simply continued to be the people they had always been and treat their sons as they had always done—but their sons changed. The boys' reaction at this turning point ranged from irritation, anger or defiance, to disregard, resigned but impatient tolerance or, in some fortunate cases, respect. Whichever form it took, the end result was a fairly rapid emotional and physical separation. Indeed, the degree of remoteness between mother and son was seen as a mark of the boy's maturity.

Too much mother emotionally? Smother love perhaps? The testimony of most sons delivered a resounding negative. Not 'too much'. Rather, 'not enough'. Many sons of that era looked back unhappily, feeling bewildered about their relationship with their mothers. And the reason they give for that unhappiness goes beyond the comparatively lesser effects of obsessive religion, rigid morality, subservient nurturing: the recurring cry of the sons of the 1950s is that their mothers showed them no affection. They feel unloved.

The idea that these men could possibly feel unloved by their mothers is contrary to every female expectation and to widespread popular wisdom about sons of this era. Yet it was a dominant feature of what many had to say.

> *She doesn't show her feelings for me and I would have no idea whether she loves me . . . my mother gives me little in the way of love, affection and support.*

> *She never tells me she loves me and whilst I expect she would certainly claim to love* all *her children, I really have no idea whether in her heart she loves me at all.*

> *My mother is not the sort of person to show her emotions. I don't know if she loves me . . . I suppose her love is shown by the fact that she has always been there.*

Some men made a distinction between whether their mother actually did not love them, or just could not show it. Other qualities sometimes compensated for the lack of affectionate behaviour: '. . . she never outwardly displayed her love for us—few if any cuddles etc., but she was fiercely loyal'. And several said their mothers' love was manifested not by gestures, but as 'a presence' or 'vibration'.

There were sons who could appreciate the difficulties of their mother's situation, who made allowances for her, but were still troubled by feeling unloved.

> *Three of us were born during the war when my father was away for long periods, therefore Mum was involved in raising the family. She had extreme mental toughness and the ability to hold us together as a family, keep us fed and clothed on very little money. To me, as a boy, she was just there. She did not have the ability to show love. I found her emotionally unapproachable. I was a timid person who needed reassurance and, I felt, never got any. She probably felt she was [showing love] and I have* no doubt *she did her best, but my brothers and I feel the same.*

The 1950s were the tail end of a long era in Anglocentric Western society during which the disorderly display of emotions was discouraged as something vulgar, not 'the done thing'. There were gender implications too. Emotions were unmanly; boys were known to be embarrassed by them.

Over the centuries, many explanations have been advanced to women for men's emotional distance. Mothers in the 1950s accepted their sons' increasing withdrawal as 'typically masculine', a sign of the worldly purposes they were called to attend, perhaps even a step towards the chivalrous protection of the weaker sex from matters too difficult for them to comprehend. Fine-sounding sentiments which women have always been eager to believe. The reality may well be nearer to one son's claim that 'because of her narrowness . . . I learned secrecy from an early age'. The reports from other sons of their discomfort, unease, even boredom with their mother's company, are too frequent to dismiss such comments as exaggerated and rare nonsense. What if the thoughts sons hide from mothers are ones women could not bear to hear?

Many adult sons confessed that they find neither comfort nor relaxation in their mother's presence. Asked their reactions to spending time with her, their answers were explicit, forthright and mainly uncomplimentary.

Irritated; bored; impatient; uninterested; never feel at ease; in small doses; don't have the time or the inclination; only out of duty; do not feel comfortable in her presence; extremely difficult to talk; time with Mum is duty time; actually find it difficult being around her.

Daughters catch glimpses of these feelings in men, controlled but barely suppressed, shown by abrupt departure, withdrawal, or a sudden burst of physical energy. As one middle-aged man admitted: 'I must say, sometimes, my son treats his mother like I sometimes treat mine . . . short!'. Daughters observe their mothers talking to the thin air left vacant by a retreating son. They watch the older women hide from its meaning by bustling to provide scones and cakes, or do the mending, washing or ironing. In this one area, daughters straddle the sexes. They can interpret their mothers' behaviour but all too well recognise the signs in their brothers. Indeed, they often sympathise with their sibling because they too have been known to share such emotions towards their mothers. Surprisingly few make the connection between themselves as daughters and sisters on the one hand and the likely male reaction to themselves as mothers. Most would be heartbroken if this was their son.

I enjoy my mother's company in limited quantities. She was here for a holiday for six months and I was glad to see her go home. She likes to talk a lot and likes the company of her family all the time. And, of course, when she's in Australia, she's only got me and my children. I work from home and I found her presence an intrusion sometimes because she wanted to talk to me constantly. I just didn't have the time, nor the inclination to talk to her . . . As I said, she lives very close to her family. When they're not here, her conversation tends to be related mostly to them and I don't know them that well because I left home when I was quite young. She wants to rattle on about my cousin this, and my cousin that, and I don't know who she's talking about. There are wider topics . . . well, no, not really, there are general current affairs we agree on—politicians are crooked, murderers and rapists should be hung, that sort of thing. She's got no, never did have, any hobbies or

> *special interests. She's only ever been interested in her family. There's nothing that she's expert in.*

In the next breath, without noticing the contradiction, this woman's son went on to answer a question about his mother's work:

> *She worked way beyond retirement. She controlled her own laboratory, bio-tested the lab animals, absolutely loved the job. She was very good at it.*

Did she abandon that expertise in his company, perhaps believing that her only validation in his life was her maternal character? Was he ungenerous to a mother who favoured his younger brother? Or was it that age made one anxious and the other annoyed in each other's company. It would be comforting to conclude it was simply the friction of a visit which lasted too long, but this son's views are only a more explicit version of those expressed by many others.

Mothers and sons were separated by many factors including education and the gender division of labour, but the designation of emotional and family affairs as exclusively women's province created a further chasm between them. The gap is exacerbated in adult life. The emphasis on family topics to the exclusion of nearly everything else in their mothers' conversation can irritate these sons beyond belief. Understanding its origin made it no easier to tolerate. But specifically male value judgments were also very evident and they, too, worked to the women's detriment. Family relationships were 'tittle-tattle'. Would sport be 'serious'? 'I spend time with my mother out of duty. I enjoy her company in very small doses. Discussions are on lightweight tittle-tattle, involving family'. Another son was just as scathing:

> *We find it extremely difficult to talk about present-day topics and always revert to 'remember this' and 'remember that', some of which I find difficult as it is over twenty years since I left home. I have to listen to the 'Death Notices' each time as various friends, relatives or acquaintances have passed on.*

Only a generous, as well as a loving son, one who was confident that he was loved and sufficiently free of ambivalence towards his mother was able to say that he spent time with her:

. . . to provide her with an outlet for her news as she loves to let you know what is happening. I sit and just listen (sometimes while I take her for a drive) and she talks non-stop for an hour.

The situation was the same, but the attitude was kinder. Whatever the motives, however, it remained a very unequal relationship.

Despite their irritation, the men do not want to hurt their mothers. As one said, after describing time with his mother as 'duty time', 'I'm sure she would be very hurt if she knew this and I try to keep such feelings from becoming evident'. Even the harshest judgments were tempered with the wish to avoid actual hurt: 'I dislike her company. I see her from time to time and I try to be pleasant. I do not want to hurt her, but if I never saw her again, it would not greatly trouble me'.

Concealed feelings which range from hostility to plain boredom result, naturally enough, in the kind of discomfort expressed by the following son in a voice heavy with doubt.

Yes . . . I enjoyed my mother's company, but I don't know that it was in a very relaxed sense. It wasn't totally out of duty, but it was never . . . well, I won't say it wasn't comfortable. It was, *but we didn't have a lot in common. When we talked, we would discuss a number of things, but our interests tended to be a bit different.*

Ironically, marriage and their own families finally offer sons of this generation something to talk about with their mothers. Perhaps this is the reason that older women are sometimes desperate for grandchildren.

We have more in common now I have children. They create lots of talking points and chances for us all to be together. The things we mainly talk about are trivial everyday things, very rarely the meaning of life or philosophical subjects. When together, we often go for walks and look after the kids.

Beyond creating new topics of mutual interest, the arrival of family and the sight of his mother in a new role can affect a son quite profoundly.

I'm reassessing my reactions to my mother's company. Now that she's a grandmother and I appear to have settled down, she's backed off a bit and we occasionally communicate rather than chat. I have never spent time with Mum out of duty since I 'left the nest'. At fourteen I wanted to fight to defend her. At seventeen, I did—she doesn't know that. Now I am growing older, I find it easier to accept her, warts and all. I try not to psychoanalyse it too much for fear of . . . what? I don't know. Basically, since watching her with her grand-daughter, I'm reminded (subconsciously) of all the great qualities she must have had when she worked a forty-hour week then came home to raise me.

Rated second after the family as a conversational link was gardening—that pleasant, domestic occupation which tends to accompany the establishment of a home. It was frequently nominated as a topic of common interest which sons could discuss with their mothers.

I only enjoy a little of her company. We are compatible in so few ways. She tries to bring me up to date on births, deaths, marriages etc. We do talk gardening, a shared love.

And gardening featured among a couple of even more positive responses:

I enjoy my mum's company and definitely not out of duty. We talk about many things, gardening, roofing the shed, anything. Money, politics and family.

We enjoy each other's company. I quite often call in to have a cup of tea and we talk about how each other's garden is looking and what new plants she has propagated etc.

The men who unequivocally described their mothers' company as enjoyable invariably had a range of topics they discussed with her, although often it was very apparent that one party was talking and the other listening. Family matters were only one topic among many: 'everyday life, my partner and my two small daughters, football, politics and my work as a taxi driver'. Politics recurs, as do books and a man's work. Very occasionally, for this generation, there is also the enthusiasm for his mother's work or studies.

Even some mother–son pairs who had a strained, alienated relationship for many years, could eventually find pleasure in each other's company, particularly if a spouse helped the process along.

Change in the mother's personality was also a notable contributor to this kind of reconciliation.

In small doses we get on very well . . . we talk of mutual friends and acquaintances, generally ending in hilarity—She has allowed the more risque aspect of her humour to surface recently—politics, books, play Scrabble. Sometimes the sense of duty is there, but it generally changes to real fun. About once every two months . . . my aunt, an amazing woman of eighty-two, comes over for tea. These are always beaut nights; my wife (more accurately, the woman I live with) pumps them about their youth and off they go; I have discovered unknown hunks of both their pasts only recently.

Mothers' attempts to extend their conversational range beyond the family, are not always sympathetically received.

My mother regards her side of the family as a pretty wonderful group. She talks about them . . . I don't really know them, but I hear about their exploits. It's not of interest [to me]. We used to live on a small farm and we did a lot of work together on that . . . She doesn't read anymore, just the newspapers and watches a lot of trash on television. She's a bit inclined to tell me what to read. She writes on the newspapers, 'see p.14'. I brought home a book about one topic she marked, but I couldn't say I was really interested. I'm interested in the wisdom of an older person, but in the day to day, I can cut her short and say 'Look, pop into your room, like a good girl'. She doesn't seem to be offended by that.

Perhaps sensing that they were being patronised or, at least, feeling that their views deserved more respect, mothers sometimes fought back vigorously. Their sons didn't mind when the topics were impersonal.

We had a lot of heated discussions, particularly in the latter years, where she used to get so annoyed with me. She'd make a statement and I'd say, 'So what you're saying is this . . .' and she'd go beserk. 'Don't you tell me what I'm saying.' This was particularly on political topics . . . around 1975, the time of the dismissal of Whitlam.

It may be no coincidence that this was also the period when modern women first became conscious of male domination and their own right to self-assertion.

Sometimes family trauma rather than self-assertion could be the trigger to stripping away the veneer of a relationship and revealing the harsh truth beneath. Under stress from his father's heart attack and a paternal instruction to 'look after your mother', one son lost control completely, leaving his 67-year-old mother still reeling with shock some months later.

> *My son came back from the hospital and said to me. 'I told Dad I'll stay the night, but I can't talk to her because she's so boring. Her conversation is so boring. I really can't stand it. It makes me so irritable . . . I don't know how you put up with her'. My son wanted me to know. He told me: 'You drive me up the wall. All this talk about your friends and your neighbours and what you do is so boring that when we had a psychologist at school for the children I had a test run with him first and told him how I felt about you.' When I told my daughter how shocked I was, she said 'Oh yes, he told me too'. My son only came to stay for a couple of weeks, then he took something I said as justification for leaving . . . I asked him 'What would you like in a mother?'. And he said: 'I want you just the way you are, but I would like you to be more interested in me. To take more interest in what I'm doing.' He didn't ask me what* I wanted, *but I told him anyway. I said: 'I would like* you *just the way* you *are but for you take just a little interest in what I do'. And he said to me: 'I must admit I'm not interested in what you do. I know that sounds wrong, but I think you could take more interest in what I do.' And I replied: 'Even though you are not interested in me?'.*

Some of the men consciously recognised that their mothers' lack of education limited their conversation and they tried to do something about it. Most encouraged the slightest indication that their mothers wanted to stretch their intellect. Some realised that it was a way to bridge the gap between them. 'Since she mentioned the business about wanting to use her brain more, I have been trying to get her to tell me how. Then, we will go on from there.' Very likely behind the flood of mature-age students in the 1970s and 1980s, there was many an encouraging son who saw the chance for greater common ground with his mother.

In general, male children of this era made few allowances for the circumstances of their mothers' lives. Although the men described their mothers in vivid detail, with memories which were often informed by sadness or regret, their accounts lacked insight. The missing ingredient was an understanding about the impact of the society in which their mothers reared them.

Some of their female contemporaries who became feminists argue that men's blindness is deliberate. Judith Arcana asserted categorically in her book *Every Mother's Son*:

> Sons apparently do know the truth of their mothers' lives—but choose not to hold that truth in their consciousness, or recognize its meaning. Here are all these men who can see, can even describe and explain, grief in the lives of women. Are they 'typical' men? Are they like 'most men'? Can we assume that most men appreciate the struggle in their mothers' lives?[21]

Much of the evidence gathered here would answer Arcana's last question in the negative but, even so, her overall contention casts ordinary men as making an active decision to oppress. Why would sons 'choose' an attitude which makes them so unhappy? It is more likely that they, too, have been the unconscious victims of the prevailing culture.

Feminists in the 1970s rightly denounced the tendency to blame mothers and yet many feminists did just that. The mother-blaming environment created by Phillip Wylie and his 'moms' during their childhood, cast a long and pervasive shadow over both the daughters and the sons of that era. The mothers of the 1950s' generation believed that they were carrying out society's most noble dictates in providing 'good men'. It was their *raison d'etre* to rear male citizens who would uphold society's values and provide model husbands for other women. It was not their fault that society's values changed so radically nor that their best efforts are today so often misinterpreted by its male and female recipients.

But mothers are not the only losers. It is impossible not to feel equal compassion for the sons: men wound tight inside themselves with the effort to suppress, ignore, avoid the resentment, even overwhelming anger, against a loved person whose influence they believe has been so pernicious. How is it that so many could describe their mothers as 'emotionally draining', as 'stultifying' or so 'narrow' that a son 'learned secrecy from an early age'? How did mothers come to be seen as 'emotionally rigid', 'lacking affection', or 'unable to express love'? How did it happen that their sons who felt 'timid', 'frightened' or 'in need of reassurance', could find no comfort in them?

In rearing men according to men's wishes, women are being blamed for the culture's shortcomings. Mothers were raising young men who could take their place in the 'other' world, the one that they did not know because they did not experience it. Neither they, nor their sons, comprehended the effect of this fateful innocence. Sensing, but not understanding the competition and the struggle for supremacy in which their sons must participate, women tried to arm their boys with education, and with the manners and dress of the powerful. The degree to which a mother insisted her son achieve educationally, behave politely and dress neatly, the extent of her attempts to direct his future, was as often a reflection of her fear for him in this unknown arena as any thwarted need to live her own life through him. In this way, mothers tried to provide their children with the only weapons they understood.

But how could a mother at home, who was teaching her children to say 'please' and 'thank you', be expected to foresee that her son would be humiliated as a 'pansy' when he used the manners she had taught him? And how could he, in those days, find an explanation which she would understand? The gap between men and women's worlds which resulted from their separate, strictly defined roles, emphasised this hurtful discrepancy between mother and son. One man spoke for many about the sorrow of best intentions gone wrong:

> *Her desire for me to appear at my best meant that she went to embarrassing extremes so I would stand out. I was not a terribly worldly six or seven year old and I would do as I was told in situations that make me cringe even today.*

Not all relationships between the sons of the 1950s and their mothers resulted in disappointment or ambivalence. Whatever their era, women and men have the capacity to break the mould. The infinite capacity inherent in human nature can always transcend personal circumstances or restrictive social customs.

Insight and context—and the confidence of being loved—were

the distinguishing qualities of men who could write about their mother with generosity and compassion even though they had left her far behind in education, outlook and experience. And there were a few, who recalled female people rather than 'mothers', whose recollections were unreservedly joyful and loving. There was a pattern to what this group had to say. Although their mothers were married, in some instances, to particularly dominant men, and although all lived in traditionally demarcated roles, the women had the advantage of high self-esteem. Their inner confidence meant that they were not afraid to express themselves directly and forthrightly, a style which was valued by their sons. These men described their mothers as possessing the stereotypical maternal qualities, such as 'caring and concern', 'shows feelings', 'supportive', but their memories reveal that these women had also developed wide-ranging interests beyond the home: 'artistic and intellectual curiosity', 'stories from work . . . witty', 'has published a book', 'achieving her goals in life'. Their natures were recognised as 'adaptable', or they had 'broadness of outlook and knowledge', qualities which their sons celebrated. These were unusual attributes for mothers of that generation and they contributed to these men's pleasure in their mothers' company.

Less fortunate sons did not 'choose' their anguish. Many of those who participated here did so because they yearned to understand. They wanted, sometimes quite desperately, to discover, at least, compassion for their mothers and they were prepared to risk emotional pain to do so—and to share it with others who might feel the same.

> *I feel a great sadness writing about this stuff. It seems disloyal to tell the truth about my poor silly old Mum. I suppose I feel sad about having failed, too. I wanted to get through to her, to deal with her directly, person to person, to find the person behind the facade, and I have never been able to do that . . . I still find the contemplation of this relationship with my mother profoundly painful.*

4 The opposite sex

Many 'experts' have investigated, analysed and pontificated at length about the mother–son relationship. Most of them have been male and most have emphasised that the nub of the relationship is the difference in sexuality. Indeed, the pivot on which everything turns has been monotonously decreed to be the penis. No doubt the experts are often right and the penis does have special significance, but the anecdotal contributions analysed here quickly suggested that the notorious male confusion between sex and the cultural attributes of gender has masked the real issues.

Her son's sex is the first aspect of a boy child which his mother meets. At birth, his main distinguishing feature is his penis. Her awareness of his health, size, length, shape and strength will quickly follow, but his unique attribute, the feature which separates him from a daughter and from his mother's own body, is his penis. Sometimes the different sexuality between mother and son can assume such disastrous importance that it distorts the relationship. One sixty-year-old son for instance, related how his mother was so unable to accept his sex that she reared him to all intents as if he was a girl. She taught him details of menstruation and childbirth and ignored his maleness altogether.

Psychiatrist Dr John Buttsworth confirmed that, in his experience, some contemporary mothers also find their son's physical difference an obstacle to their mothering:

> Some women have feelings about men that are focused on the obviousness of 'men-ness' i.e. the penis. Seeing a penis is quite a traumatic experience for them. It often gets in the way of their desire to be affectionate to a male child. I've seen many women who come to discuss a bad relationship with their son and one part of the problem is that their son's penis 'got in the way'. They found it difficult to actually cuddle the baby. Even simple things like changing nappies were a little bit stressful because they were anxious about getting into close contact with the penis. It's not actually the sex. It's the penis of the son which interferes with the relationship. Of course, the reverse is also true. There are women who are very turned on by masculinity so they really enjoy cuddling their sons. Those boys are endowed with a lot of love and they're the ones who grow up and relate well to women in later life.[22]

Until the recent past, women's acquaintance with male sexuality could be extremely limited. When parents concealed their bodies from children, when adult sex was often conducted in the dark, and printed or graphic sex information could only be found in the remotest corners of libraries, it was quite feasible that a mother had never actually seen a penis before having a son. He might provide her first real opportunity to inspect one with undisguised curiosity. When the other sex was such an alien being, it is not surprising that blatant male sexuality could generate emotions in a mother ranging anywhere from dismay or fear to surprise, pride, fascination or nervousness.

No one was more likely to feel trepidation at the prospect of having a son than a woman whose family lacked men. Some women who grew up in all-female families had no acquaintance with men at all. They found the idea of just having a male around unusual, let alone giving birth to one. In some cases, the possibility of having a boy never occurred to them and they were caught by surprise when it happened. Some were shocked. A few were devastated. More commonly, they thought about it in advance and waited nervously, worrying that their inexperience with men would make them unable to manage as the mother of boys. Mixed with their doubt was enormous excitement. Growing up without males could just as easily create a tremendous longing for a boy. A 63-year-old woman said: 'I always wanted sons and grandsons because I grew up in a fatherless family and had no contact with male relatives at all'. When a woman with no experience of men at all in her own family married a man from a culture that revered males, as in the following case, the birth of a boy was an extraordinary and wonderful event.

When my son was born, I was very conscious he was male. And very proud of it. I was also very aware that I had no experience with men, so I guess I was a bit naive in his whole upbringing. Having a boy child was such a special thing. I saw him as so special. My husband was away and I had him on my own for the first fifteen months of his life. My life revolved around him. (mother 54, son 27)

In all-female families, the arrival of a baby boy brought joy and wonderment amounting almost to reverence. Lying in a hospital bed nearly forty years ago, Angela watched her mother inspect her first grandson.

> *Our family was predominantly female as my mother's had been before that . . . The morning after the birth of my little son, Mother was with me, fussing as usual, fixing the pillows, waiting eagerly to see the baby as the cot was wheeled in. He was awake, crossing his eyes and making funny shapes with his mouth. I watched my mother looking at him silently, pulling back the covers. I noticed her curious expression. At length, she spoke, and I've never forgotten her words . . . 'He's . . . he is so different. He's nothing like our little girl. I mean, he's so lean looking . . . well, he just doesn't look like your baby at all! (age 63)*

Angela's own feelings were also affected by the novelty and glory of bearing the only male baby in a family who were perpetually emphasising and celebrating her feat.

> *Although it was a great joy to see my two baby daughters, the joy of seeing my baby son was* tinged with pride as well *(her emphasis). Maybe it was the family's reaction: an aunt who was beside herself at having a boy at last, a granny who exclaimed with awe and rapturously-clasped hands 'At last, at last' there was a grandson to 'carry on the name'. Also in childhood, I expected boys would be like daddy and girls would be like mummy and I grew up scared of boys. To this day I can see the spectre of a particularly fearsome one . . . who was repeatedly chasing little girls into the air-raid shelters to pull down their pants . . . And I still tremble when I remember hiding while this creature bashed up our little boy cousin. Yet, in my son, I saw the rare, golden glow of maleness at its best; I saw it also in my husband, but did not feel any particular pride about it, but I never associated my husband with my general unease pertaining to the opposite sex . . . Sometimes, I felt a vague uneasiness and self-searching about the love I felt for my son which was different to the love I felt for my husband, daughters and mother. Over the years, I suspect that my husband mildly resented this love which my boy baby had released within me, but fortunately, he always made his love for me and the children very apparent.*

Social change in Western society has reduced the cultural worship of boy babies and a less prudish reaction to sex and nudity means that the sexuality of a male child is less likely to discomfort a woman now, but John Buttsworth's experience clearly demonstrates that some mothers still find male sex organs confronting. And the response of women with little direct experience of males has remained very similar. From this study it is obvious that some contemporary mothers reacted in the same way as mothers would have forty years ago. Growing up without males in the family proves more influential in how they feel about having a boy than the modern cultural and social context in which they live. Lacking the background of prosaic daily contact which turns men into fallible human beings, they tend to romanticise the male child they have borne. Their idea of him is based entirely on gender stereotypes.

> *I even found it hard being married because I'd never had to cope with a male. I never thought I'd be the mother of a boy. Once I was pregnant, I imagined he would be a boy, but for years and years before that, I could only ever see myself as the mother of a girl. A lot of my friends want the frills, the laciness, the prettiness of a daughter. Thank God, I don't have to cope with that because I'm not a fiddly person. It's really good that Dean can be a little grubby . . . (but) he wasn't born particularly boisterous in a traditional boyish way, and he was always very affectionate. I held him for ten months, because everytime I put him down, he cried. (mother 40, son 5)*

Very few women today would come to mother a boy without ever having seen a penis. Widespread sex education from an early age in schools and information in easily-accessible media or books, ensure that most girls are at least acquainted with diagram drawings, if not with actual photographs or experience of the real thing. Perceptions—or experience—of sexual violence may shape a younger woman's attitude negatively, but simple ignorance would rarely be the cause. Although a baby's penis may still be intriguingly different from his mother's own body, it is far less likely to be so alien that it makes a woman feel unable to cope. Nevertheless, sexuality can go astray between mothers and sons, particularly if the mother fails to set boundaries which create an appropriate sexual distance between them. Without definition the relationship can become more like that of lovers than of parent and child. The participants in such an unbalanced partnership are often totally oblivious to the problem, even though an observer finds it blindingly obvious.

Visiting relatives inter-State, I was embarrassed at the extremely 'affectionate' relationship between a cousin and her eighteen-year-old son, embarrassed to say the least. An elderly aunt who had lived with them for years, also seemed agitated, even hostile. Eventually, she snapped very disapprovingly at the son: 'Leave your mother alone and go get yourself a girlfriend!' It was all out in the open, but the mother didn't appear to see anything unusual. (age 64)

The greatest taboo in Western society is mother–son incest, but incestuous acts by women do occur and a small number of these are between mother and son. Professionals working in this area presently believe that they are very rare, although there is some concern that incidents are under-reported. However, frankness about the subject has only developed in the last twenty years and information concerning the sexual abuse of sons requires men to start talking about it.

Sons who have been victims of incest experience the same legacy of guilt as daughters, but it appears centred on the degree to which they felt they co-operated. Their guilt is exacerbated by their enjoyment. Describing his experience years later, a middle-aged man told *The Bulletin*:

My mother never forced me. She always asked . . . I thought I was the perpetrator. It was an enormous adventure, a secret, not like a girl being raped. There was pleasure and guilt mixed. Years later, I felt terrible guilt because I thought I could have said no.[23]

The relationship between most mothers and sons never comes anywhere near incest. The majority of women reported that they were close to oblivious of their child's different sex in their daily lives, only reminded occasionally if something brought it to their attention. Generally, their boys were children who just happened to be male. Psychologist Rudi Guerra commented that some degree of awareness is perfectly normal.

Being conscious of your children's sexuality is part of parenthood.

> It is whether you act on it or not that matters. If you go round verbalising your feelings, I think it would be a matter of concern, but the feeling is natural.[24]

But some mothers do worry. As adolescence approaches, they increasingly wonder what is appropriate behaviour around their son. Even those who have been unselfconscious about nudity around the house can become unsure of when, or if, to conceal their bodies. Their concern was more often expressed as the effect of *their* nudity on their son rather than the reverse which, as much as anything, reveals the degree of anxiety still generated by Freudian theories about 'seductive' mothers.

The professionals are unaminous about how mothers should react to their sons' developing sexuality. John Buttsworth commented:

> Good mothering is being in tune with the feelings of your child. There are no rules. A mother will pick up her son's feelings. If he's embarrassed, she'll sense it. And similarly, she'll pick up her own feelings if she's watching him with no clothes on. It is a matter of attunement of feelings. And of respecting the feelings of the child. If he's embarrassed, don't look. Or show him respect and cover up. It's not necessarily an issue for talking over. My first approach is to respect the feelings.[25]

Mutual respect was the approach many mothers chose. As their son reached the age of twelve or thirteen, they began to knock on his door before entering, if it was not already wide open. They shut bathroom doors or flung on a dressing gown before rushing through the house. In return, they expected the same discretion from their boys. It was a question of privacy as well as respect. But not everyone made this kind of transition easily. For some women it was always a subject fraught with uncertainty and confusion. A few found it titillating.

Their sons' sexuality was a significant element in their relationship for two participating mothers who reared boys during the 1970s and 1980s. Believing that sexuality was something that must be taught, one woman made sexual behaviour and sexual attitudes prominent issues during her children's primary years, but she emphasised how parents of either sex must change their behaviour when the children reached adolescence. She took care to point out that she had always been aware that 'mothers have to keep a certain distance from their sons in their teens especially so they mature properly in a masculine way', but, strangely, her attitudes extended only to public displays and did not include notions of her personal withdrawal and privacy.

> *My husband loved to 'stalk' round naked and that was fine before the female hormones began developing in our daughter. But there comes a time of growing awareness and parents need to pull back, otherwise some of the wonderful mystique of sex is spoilt. And when our children's friends were in our house they were embarrassed by such behaviour. I had quite a battle on this one. With my son, I did not openly display myself when he moved into his teens. When he wanted to see me, he would open the door of the shower and unashamedly stare! (age 51)*

The problems for another single mother during this period arose when her ten-year-old son's teacher rang to warn that the boy's affectionate nature was attracting homosexual advances from a friend. Alarmed at the idea, his mother not unnaturally hurriedly agreed with the suggestion that she must tell him not to be demonstrative. The consequences to the boy's self-image and to their relationship were predictable. From then on, sex and gender developed along rigidly stereotyped lines which during adolescence became a serious aggravation in their relationship.

> *He was very affectionate and sensitive as a child, always caring, but he had to learn to show less affection around the age of ten because this is a conditioning of the outside world . . . At puberty, he was 'overnight' embarrassed to see me in the nude. This has never been discussed because of his embarrassment. During adolescence, he developed his father's mannerisms, although he had not been exposed to them . . . but he always listened, and never seriously opposed me, until the day I found 'porn' magazines under his bed. When I started spouting off, he stood up to me in a different way. He was right and I was wrong. It made quite an impression on me. In my eyes he became a 'man' overnight . . . I believe it's very important to show affection and I would like to have been more affectionate as I feel it is very natural within me*

but I had to hold back. I'm not sure why. Maybe because of his embarrassment. (mother 47, son 24)

Women absorb masculinity's messages about 'mummy's boys'. Most are also aware of Freud's theories about seductive mothers even if they do not know their origin. The anxiety that they might 'make' their son homosexual hovers in the minds of many of them. Such concern is not surprising when the risk they are said to pose is frequently brandished at them. Women who reared sons in the last twenty-five years could be targets for the same male attitudes as their counterparts in an earlier era. Mothering in a different social climate, during an era which boosted women's self-esteem, meant the criticism might be slightly less virulent—and the women more confident to dilute it with their own judgment—but they could still be severely shaken.

A mother in her forties, whose son was born in 1970, faced heavy pressure from her husband to ensure that his son was reared in an appropriately 'masculine' way.

My husband was in the Army so perhaps the pressure to be macho was even greater. The fear of turning out a 'mummy's boy', a son who was gay, was even worse in that atmosphere. In England twenty years ago to be gay was a deformity blamed on the mother. I suspect little has changed . . . So the cuddling had to stop. It is a difficult time when relationships are going to be strained anyway and there is a need to reassure the rebellious teenager that you love him, even if you don't like him very much. A quick hug goes a long way here. But it is deemed unsuitable for mothers to hug young men, especially their offspring. This is one of the areas in which I was criticised, for always being too demonstrative with him . . . How do you replace the cuddles? (mother 46, son 24)

One way or the other women learn that they are a potential threat to their sons' sexuality. The homophobic fears of individual fathers are a major source of this concern. The folklore passed on by other mothers adds to the pressure. So do the recycled Freudian theories which still permeate the popular culture. As recently as 1992, the idea was propagated yet again in the popular media by the comments of a well-known single mother, whose son was still an infant. '. . . I worry all the time that I'm on the wrong track.

I'm bossy by nature and I might be too overpowering and he'll be queer and it'll be all my fault . . .'[26]

Men refused to believe that mothers might fear 'creating' a homosexual son. It was very obvious that they could not begin to imagine the effect which their own attitudes and the wider male culture had on others. The scorn of one 48-year-old son was fairly typical. He dismissed the suggestion that mothers felt that way as ridiculous.

> *Perhaps it's just that mothers don't know how to handle their sons. Maybe they're naturally intimidated by them in the sense that they're different—they're a man—and the female tends to be a bit more submissive, while the man is more 'outwards'. And they argue. I think it [any distancing] is more to do with the upbringing of boys and girls. You tend to be a lot more protective of daughters than sons. (age 48)*

His attitude had been formed by his own circumstances and in particular by the examples of his strong, decisive, unemotional mother who confidently dominated the family while his mild-mannered, retiring father happily spent his life absorbed in his work. Without realising that it was the only issue on which he described his father as intervening, his son clearly remembered paternal pressure to conform to appropriate masculine behaviour.

> *I'm quite sure my mother's attitude to homosexuality would be 'So, what else is news?'. It wouldn't have upset her one iota. It wouldn't have worried her. It would have worried my father. He would have gone off his brain. He carried on all the time . . . 'Boys don't wear ties. Boys don't have hats on . . .'. He would have gone right off about homosexuality.*

Women recognise their guilty fear of 'making' a homosexual and will discuss it quite readily. Men find the idea incredible. A homosexual son recognised the existence of fear and the dangers posed by homophobia, but he also denied that his own mother would ever have worried in this way.

> *Fear is an important issue, for all sides. Fear of 'creating' a homosexual son is usually generated by men who, in my opinion, are actually reacting to their own insecurities. Threatened masculinity is a most dangerous thing as any bashed wife will*

attest. Ignorance, as usual, drives the fear . . . My father is a typical male product of his era in his homophobia, but Mum isn't. She has been perhaps more emotive towards my (straight) younger brother, but he is the youngest in the family and had to handle the farm from a very young age so he needed her special support. I don't believe that Mum has ever worried about 'creating' a homosexual son, but is worried that she may (does) have one. A big difference. (age 28)

The following description from a mother whose son *is* homosexual, contains everything that men predict, women fear and homosexuals themselves deny as being the 'cause' of their sexuality. A single factor may never be identified as the reason for male homosexuality. It may never be conclusively demonstrated whether a particularly close relationship between mother and son is cause—or effect—or totally irrelevant. Nevertheless, Wanda's story is the sad recital of a mother who loved not wisely, but too well.

Born in Romania, Wanda fled the advancing Russians to Germany where she married an Estonian refugee. They migrated to Australia and were among the first group of 'displaced persons' after World War II. Now approaching seventy years of age, she lives alone in a rural area, describing herself as 'very crafty'—into pottery, weaving, spinning and basketmaking. Her son is now thirty-eight years of age, her daughter, two years younger.

My son the miracle . . . After many years of marriage, we dearly wanted a child. We went to a sterility clinic and a son was born to us, Paul. My husband worked in Newcastle and I stayed in Sydney devoting my life, my time, to my son. It was a miracle. I could not believe it. After several miscarriages, a daughter, then no more.

We had a perfect life: two children, a house, even a dog. Paul could do no wrong. Moved to Newcastle—bigger house, garden. I loved my son, almost possessed. My friends warned me, I am showing it. Be careful. And so life went on—bigger house, better position, promotion, big steps for a new Australian. Then my husband was advised to re-enter university, study Economics. He did that at night . . . This took up all his time and left the children's upbringing to me.

Paul was lovely, helpful, caring. He was Mummy's boy. We did a lot together. (He was) always ready to help. Then to high school, competition, and in 4th form, a scholarship. (My) husband had no time even for congratulations. Too busy . . . About this time we held a New Year party. My guest arrived minus her husband, but with her son. He was clothed in an army coat, bulging with a bottle. And 'pot'. We were too blind to see all this. End of my lovely son.

He made aeroplane models, closed doors, burned candles to dry the paint, funny smells, trouble at school, truancy most weeks. My husband is always too busy. I am too weak. One day I met my son in town with a car load of drop-outs. Big reckoning, lots of lies, lots of promises. We should have seen the writing on the wall, but how blind can you get. He finished his HSC, failed. His job in industry was no good. Started his own audio business. Drugs, police arrest for smoking pot. My husband did his best with a bond, too late. And you know, we never talked. Like a taboo. He straightened out through meditation, got his own house and a new boyfriend. Now, this should be a warning, but not us, stupid parents. Oh no. One boyfriend after another and we now realise he is gay.

In all this time I love him and gave him any help he needed. Not his father. He was too involved in his work, degree etc.

I would never want my son to be like my husband. God forbid. Our life was so lovely while we were young and doing things together my daughter and he—*the picnics, swims and outings, which all finished when he started to study and get on. We all suffered, I am sure, as there was no father, no man or adviser. Just make money, save, buy and progress. We lost each other then. We lost the man in the family. The son lost him too.*

Now I enjoy my son more than ever. Even so, we see each other not often, but when he comes, always late, he brings me little things, like fruit, or a promise, or like the other day, a complaint about his new love who he called 'a slut', who took him for all he had. (By the way, I lent him the thousand dollars for a holiday for the two of them.) My daughter, after two divorces, got a new young lover. (She is) not very nice to me. Her advice was to book into a retirement village and do not count on her for help. Amen. My husband died. I am alone. Happy. Healthy. And I love them both, really . . . I think . . .

Wanda's story contains the classic Freudian ingredients for the creation of a homosexual: a 'mummy's boy', a hostile relationship with the father, a strong, close involvement with the mother. But the popular assumptions are far too facile. The stereotype requires closer examination. Brent Waters, Professor of Child Psychiatry at the University of New South Wales commented:

> That kind of family has been blamed for just about everything . . . for a long time homosexuality was supposed to be due to being reared by a very over-protective mother and either an absent or psychologically absent father. My view is that that particular configuration of parents can give rise to all kinds of problems with children's development, but also, that some of those families do fine. People judge the stereotypes. It is very easy to speculate second and third-hand. You need to get into the family to know what is going on beneath the surface.[27]

Psychologist Rudi Guerra agreed, describing popular theories about mother's threat to their sons' sexuality as nothing but myths.

> Perhaps a boy could be influenced to appear effeminate, but that doesn't mean he'd be homosexual. And if a mother never comforted her son and always encouraged him to be tough that's no guarantee that he wouldn't grow up to be homosexual either.[28]

The son whose mother brought him up like a girl, teaching him about menstruation and childbirth rather than ejaculation and erections, was amazed that he had turned out heterosexual. A homosexual son was insistent that mothers played no part.

> *No one, mothers included, has made us gay. It is true that most of us are closer to our mothers than fathers, but only because we find it hard to relate to the straight male lifestyle. To be blunt, it is unfulfilling. Blame is often pushed onto mothers by fathers who are unable to cope and believe their son's homosexuality to be a slur on their (own) masculinity. (age 27)*

The verdict is undecided on the contentious subject of whether homosexuals are born or made although research is increasingly favouring the former. It does, at least, seem clear-cut that male sexual orientation and the external attributes of masculinity are quite separate. Whether or not a boy has the outward appearance of being a 'sissy' or a 'real' boy is immaterial. Neither will ultimately determine whether or not he turns out to be homosexual. And a mother's loving hug for a teenage son should be confidently given, and comfortably reciprocated, without the condemnation of the boy's peers—or his father.

But as long as masculinity remains oppressive, mothers and sons will worry unnecessarily. In *Men, Sex and Other Secrets*, author Peter McMillan briefly but vividly described the secret anxiety which is almost certainly shared by many adolescent boys. After years of abuse at school for being a mummy's boy, including being derisively nicknamed 'Patricia' by his peers because of his effeminate mannerisms, Peter had more specific reasons than most to dread what adolescent sexuality would reveal to him. He left school deeply relieved of his greatest fear.

> By the time I finished school, I had managed to become as apparently male as anybody else in my all-male school. I would inform people that I had not suffered in any way by lacking a father. My teenage terror that I might suddenly discover I was homosexual (which I assumed would be like suddenly discovering I was doomed with a fatal disease) had not been realised.[29]

Telling their families is an enormous hurdle for gay men and some consider suicide rather than risk their families' condemnation. Many postpone telling their parents indefinitely, choosing instead to suffer the insecurity and limitations imposed by hiding such a secret.

> *What makes it hard is that we haven't actually discussed my sexuality so I don't entirely know how my parents feel. One thing that has always stood out is a comment of Mum's made when we were in the garden alone just talking. I was about 21. 'If any of you should turn out to be homosexual, I wouldn't exactly be pleased but I would try to accept the fact.' In a way I feel sorry that I didn't have the confidence then (or now for that matter) to open right up to her. I just wasn't ready to cope. Should she offer me that opening again, I'd take it. It was said as an aside. I hope that she was telling me things'd be OK . . . Keeping my parents, and Mum in particular, blocked out of a significant part of my life is cheating each of us but I am not sure I have the strength to endure the confession . . . I have never lost a friend in someone who learns afterwards that I am gay. It should give me faith in myself as a person, but it fails me in my own family. (age 28)*

Sadly, this son's fear is not unusual, or unreasonable. Too often, homosexuals who tell their families are rejected or abused in just the way that they dread. For every parent who is able to receive the news, at least with resignation if not delight, there are others, particularly fathers, who react with violent disgust.

> *Two of my son's school mates were gay and he was appalled and angry when one of the fathers bashed the daylights out of his boy over this revelation. (age 51)*

If mothers can acquire the confidence to trust their judgment despite the dominant male culture, and despite the likely homophobic reactions of their partners, then they might be able to ease the isolation of a terrified adolescent who is realising for the first time with a mixture of fascination and excitement, fear and self-disgust, that what 'turns him on' is not girls. As one man pointed out so tellingly, 'No sane person would choose to be gay'. For a teenager in the middle of intense peer pressure to conform, who despite any existing conflict probably desperately yearns for his father's approval, the discovery that he is different must be devastating. There can be little joy in the recognition of how he feels, for he knows it will bring down abuse and anger and rejection upon him.

The debate will continue about 'the cause' of homosexuality. It may never be settled. In the interim, too many women are made to feel nervous about their influence on their sons. The theory that they are the weakness which can undermine their sons' sexuality is still so prevalent that many perfectly sensible women, doing a perfectly straightforward job of rearing their male children, have this nagging uncertainty at the back of their minds. It comes to the fore as the boys approach adolescence and it undermines mothers' confidence. Women will benefit from recognising how much of the pressure arises from fearful masculinity.

5 Learning to be a man

Mothers contribute to boys' difficulties by not understanding the process of becoming a man. To survive the requirements of masculinity, their sons learn to split themselves in two between the defensive facade and the real person underneath. Women's mistake is to think that it is a romantic compliment that only they should be allowed to know the inner man. In fact, it is a severe defect of masculinity. Unless mothers break through this traditional assumption and clarify what masculinity means, they will continue to blunder in their sons' world.

From the moment boys enter the school playground, they struggle to survive the 'put downs' of their peers. Colloquially, this translates into a philosophy of 'beat or be beaten' which can take either a verbal or physical form. Women catch glimpses of this without realising its devastating implications. One mother participating in this project innocently described the advice her father gave his children, which she had passed on to her son. 'Never be walked on. Never eat dirt. Never be cornered. Look, you will find a way out.' It was the prescription of a man who had spent his life braced against attack.

Boys assault one another physically and verbally for not being 'male' enough, for being like girls, or for being 'sissies' or 'wusses'. It is the beginning of sexism. The threat of being like a girl, or an inadequate male, a mummy's boy or sissy, is the weapon which enforces conformity to the masculine 'norm'. Boys' conditioning is essentially negative—the need to demonstrate masculinity by not being feminine, to prove it even further by not being a lesser male. Paul Whyte, a men's therapist, points out that such severe conditioning limits the kind of boy you can be:

> . . . you are abused and abused and abused until anything resembling qualities associated with girls, 'poofters', 'wimps' etc. is hidden. These include all the qualities needed for easy interaction with other human beings. It is a choice that every male makes to survive the culture. Later on, any time a man leaves the conditioned male role, he is subject to anti-gay abuse irrespective of his sexual preference. It is not surprising that men feel like their life is threatened if their manhood is called into question.[30]

The tough culture which conditioned boys in the 1950s has not vanished. The struggle for supremacy may be less overt, at least among the middle class, but it is still pervasive. The pressure to be men, not to be like girls, not a 'wuss', still exists. A thirteen-year-old girl made this plain with her description of the strife experienced by her nine-year-old cousin:

> *He adores his mother and ignores everyone who teases him because he plays with girls at school. But he is not abnormal . . . He wants to be like his mother. But be a man. I think he would grow up to be a great boy if people did not tease and mock him so much that he can't make any good friends.*

Physical strength is often the only response which works for boys in the testing environment of primary school. Paul Whyte emphasised the importance of allowing them to practise being tough rather than leaving them vulnerable and exposed.

> When a boy starts kindergarten, he's dropped without any warning into a 'beat or be beaten' culture among the other males. Little boys have to figure out how to hit back in the right way, otherwise they're either beaten or friendless. They need to play a lot of rough games just to figure out every permutation on violence and what it means . . . It's their attempt to tussle with what's happening to them . . . It's completely misunderstood. If you stop them they don't get the chance to work it out. They just get beaten up.[31]

The popular interpretation of a boy's resort to physical aggression is that it is an innate violence which should be eradicated but, in the mid-1980s, Tony Eardley, writing in *The Sexuality of Men*, argued that male sexuality is not violent in any biological sense, but a consequence of the way masculinity is constructed in our society.

> . . . research into domestic violence and rape suggests that batterers and rapists are not necessarily specially disturbed, come from all walks of life, and in most respects are ordinary men. What does come out clearly in the Dobash pioneering work, for example, is that the wider the gulf between a man's notion of proper masculine character and behaviour and his own perceptions of himself, the more likely he is to be violent.[32]

The implications for mothers of sons are that a boy needs to feel confidently masculine *before* he can abhor violence, rather than the other way round. Suddenly, the well-recognised phenomenon of 'the gentle giant' becomes comprehensible rather than a contradiction in terms. Even if he does not know how to throw a punch, a large man is safe from attack by other males purely through the presumed power of his size. He does not need to prove it. Paul Whyte recommends that mothers should encourage their boys to study the martial arts, where they will gain the confidence of strength and the ability to demonstrate it if necessary, along with a philosophy of self-disciplined physical power.

If these are the dynamics of a growing boy's environment, it explains why a twelve-year-old boy confided revealingly: 'I always have enjoyed my mother's company because, unlike when I'm with my friends, I don't have to watch every word I say and can relax a bit'.

A mother's company can offer safe refuge, but in the playground, life is a daily round of social interaction which can be violent or, at the very least, *does* violence to a boy's tender feelings. Mothers watch it and try to make sense of what is happening. Carefully, they rationalise the contradictions which confront them, but their confusion is revealed when they see the difference between the boy they know and the boy they see with his peers. Nor do they perceive the socialisation pressures displayed in a 'short-tempered' boy who 'likes to correct you'.

> *My son is eight. He is a fairly strong-willed boy and can be quite stubborn. However, at school he would appear to be more reserved and certainly not the leader of the pack. But he won't do anything if he doesn't choose to. He is very quick to pick up mistakes. He likes to correct you. He used to be quite short-tempered but this isn't so obvious as he gets older. He is very adaptable and bright, enjoys his schoolwork and also greatly enjoys sports. He claims to like playing football, but in practice is quite nervous of contact sports. He doesn't seem to be quite the typical 'rough' boy, but has a gentler nature. He won't hurt an animal ever. Emotionally, he seems on par with others of his age, although I feel he is less mature than my daughters were at his age.*

Oblivious to the nature of the struggle their son is experiencing in the playground, mothers of boys wait in vain for them to bring home a 'best friend' from primary school. Unaware that the boy's reluctance to socialise is a symptom of his need to rest from the pressures of masculinity, mothers try to help the process through well-meaning arrangements with other mothers, or by urging him to invite friends home. The boys co-operate, but rarely initiate any follow-up. Their lack of enthusiasm baffles their mothers. It is not a pattern women recognise.

In any gathering of mothers of young boys, a faint anxiety can be detected. It is betrayed in deceptively casual exchanges about their sons' friends. They are checking whether it is only their boy who appears isolated. Mothers are puzzled at their sons' apparent disinterest in 'making friends' because they don't understand how masculine culture differs from feminine culture. Daughters search out kindred spirits. Sons find protectors, or allies, followers or antagonists and, out of the defensive strategies of masculinity, they relate to their peers for what they offer rather than who they are. Unlike girls, for whom a best friend is a status symbol, if boys pair off it is a sign of exclusion—they have failed to find a place in the hierarchy. It is also a risk. In the rush to masculinity, even eight-year-olds can and will level a charge of 'poofter'.

The development of 'masculinity' is not a charming, rough but loveable process, although it is often presented that way. Under its veneer, it is, even today, survival of the fittest. The following description of boys and girls by a 35-year-old mother who is also a teacher, contained all the features of a familiar, because widely held, view. Its perspective disguises the unpalatable aspects of developing masculinity.

> *I rather like little boys. They're just a nice balance. Sometimes with girls you get that cattiness, the bitchiness, which the boys counterbalance nicely. They tend to have fisticuffs, then it's all over . . . There's a notable difference how boys and girls relate. I think girls can be a lot nastier. The boys tend to be a bit more physical, but they don't tell tales or call names quite so much. It's a generalisation, but something I've observed over many years.*

The flavour of this description constructs its meaning. Presented in these terms, little boys appear charming, while girls are quite unattractive. Without changing the facts, another angle puts a different complexion on the scene. In their concentration on personal attributes—'bitchiness'—and the reaction generated by 'telling tales', perhaps girls are practising relationships: learning how emotions are created and how they feel. And any knowledge of the dynamics of masculinity suggests that the boys' rough-and-ready fisticuffs are not as simple, or as appealing, as they seem. Certainly, their easy resolution requires disregard for others' feelings, rather than emotional awareness.

The extent to which women fail to comprehend the male culture was demonstrated by the collective hopes which the mothers in this study held for the qualities that they would like their sons to develop. A combination of 'thoughtful, kind, considerate and caring' were the traits they nominated and these ranked equally with the standard masculine attributes of 'independence' and 'self-reliance', but were way out in front of any other qualities. These are valid aspirations, but very feminine, and noticeably incompatible with the construction of masculinity as it currently exists. Only when mothers understand the nature of the culture which opposes their hopes will they be able to play their part as agents for change. Their love and feminine 'instinct' are not enough. This campaign requires insight and strategy.

A mother whose son is now twenty-four, confessed her bewilderment when she thought back over his childhood.

> *Boys always dislike girls,* why? *When my son was around ten or twelve, his headmistress phoned me and asked me to have a word with him because a lad who was known to have homosexual tendencies was making advances to him. He was innocently responding to the affectionate gestures. This was a shock to me and I was most grateful that the headmistress had the insight and concern to contact me. I can understand a friendly boy responding to an affectionate 'pat on the back'—at this age, for some reason, girls are taboo and most boys learn to hide their affectionate nature especially with their mothers because it is seen to be 'sissy'. I think it's important to understand why boys and girls hate each other at this age. (age 42)*

Traditionally, mothers' predominant reaction to masculine culture has been to comply with its requirements. A major issue has always been masculinity's demand that 'big boys don't cry'. In the 1950s, most mothers reinforced this unquestioningly. It will never be known how many actually believed in it, and how many simply complied in order to help their boys survive. Certainly, some younger mothers who continued the traditional conditioning have regretted it with hindsight. Ann's boy was a teenager during the late 1970s. 'One of my biggest regrets is when my son was around fourteen—he used to kiss me goodbye—and I told him he was too big for that. (age 53)

A new generation has the confidence to risk making changes. Some mothers of boys under twelve are exploring different ways of balancing their child's nature with the masculine culture. Acting from strong convictions about non-violence, as well as the contemporary emphasis on the need for boys to express their emotions, some mothers in this study even considered it worth the risk of isolating their sons from their peers. They took a personal stand against the masculine tradition and, when they were supported by their partners, this resolution could permeate their entire child-rearing.

> *Our boys are 12 and 10. We have brought them up to choose what* they *want to be, not what boys should do. They have chosen not to go to soccer or footie. Rob, age 12, played cricket for a few seasons, but likes to be home on Saturday. They both did judo for two years and advanced several belts. They stopped because of the tournaments where screaming parents yelled 'Get him! Kill him!' Their coach said with more killer instinct they could become black belts. Killer instinct? So, Luke sails with his Dad, Rob runs (but not with a club). They both learn music and Rob also draws and sings. Sissy? Not on your life. Caring—yes! . . . We have encouraged them to be themselves. They don't cry much any more, but they used to, and I have* never *said 'boys don't cry'. (age 40)*

A younger mother in her mid-thirties was more pragmatic than idealistic. Very conscious of the roughhouse playground environment which awaited her five-year-old boy, she tried to find a compromise which took account of the still dominant masculine culture but did not encourage sexist attitudes. Her dilemma was typical of other mothers who were trying to raise non-sexist boys without jeopardising their masculine status. In the absence of any real discussion on the subject, she was left like many others to do the best she could.

> *It's a dilemma because my elder son has a tendency to break into tears if he falls over. I'm having to say, 'Don't do that'. I don't say 'They'll call you a sissy'. I say, 'Don't scream and cry. I'm really sorry, but don't carry on'. And I'm really pummelling that into him because he'll get beaten to a pulp with things like that. You've got to impose some of those stereotypes. I avoid telling him 'It's babyish. Kids will laugh at you etc.'. I just say that when Mummy or Daddy hurt themselves, they say 'ouch', but they don't cry and carry on.*

Better understanding of masculinity's features will allow mothers to develop more effective mechanisms for helping their boys cope. Awareness that, for boys, school is not a matter of making friends and being kind and thoughtful to them, but more a case of staying 'one up' on the next fellow, will enable mothers to identify the symptoms such as bravado, incessant posturing and the struggle to appear invulnerable. Masculine culture will become explicable in the wariness with which some boys react to others, the reluctance to make an approach which, to an uncomprehending mother, seems such a simple matter. Fathers know why small boys tag along with big ones but most adult men, at present, will tend to confirm the status quo rather than seek ways to change it. Even a woman with a partner who supports less rigid forms of masculinity must still help her son find a compromise between the old and the new. Mothers who understand male culture could develop real judgment about when and how to stand against it and when to be simply, but knowingly, supportive. They would know how to relate to their sons in terms the boys find genuinely helpful.

Addressing boys' early need for physical strength, Paul Whyte commented:

> Most mothers try to get sons to be as soft and loving as they can, not realising what they're doing is pulling the rug out from under the boys so they'll get beaten up even more when they go to school. Sons figure this out and figure the mums have betrayed them. They need a lot of love as a person, but (also) consideration of their need to be tough and fight because until

> they can do that they can't relate across the male population. They're at risk.[33]

Mothers struggle with a dilemma that goes against their instincts. A woman whose son was only eight articulated her growing uncertainty.

> *I felt thrilled to have a son. However, I treated him pretty much as my daughters regarding toys, handling him etc. He's older now and I have encouraged him to stand up for himself, but never to be a bully or fighter. I've found it more difficult with a son than I did with daughters in dealing with this aspect of life. I don't want my son to be 'weak' and dominated. It's acceptable for a girl to keep out of fights and not be 'tough', but more difficult for a boy. As he's getting older, I'm encouraging him to be fair, honest, a good sport and prepared to 'have a go'. At present, I would say the early toddler years were the easiest. (age 39)*

A possible middle course between a mother's wishes and the current needs of masculinity is to help a boy understand the difference between his reality and his facade. In this way, a mother validates his inner nature—this is at least a compromise arrangement until more fathers make a distinction between maleness and masculinity and can give their sons the crucial validation of an adult male. In the interim, while not throwing out the masculine survival techniques, a boy's mother can ensure that he keeps track of how he really feels underneath and can see the posturing for what it should be—just a defensive tactic until he grows up. As Paul Whyte said:

> They [the boys] only ever need to *appear* to conform. Mothers can help them appear to be violent, but they don't have to actually *be* violent. There's a huge difference. You have to be able to act tough. Boys understand that.

It is a fine line of difference to understand, but recognising its existence might make it easier for women to avoid giving their sons advice which the boys know is unrealistic. Contributions from sons of all ages made it clear that inappropriate advice from their mothers is one of the greatest sources of sons' ambivalence towards them; it affects respect, trust and intimacy. It contributes to the derogatory view males hold of females.

Boys' experience with their own peer group has another implication for mothers. If they spend their days struggling for supremacy with other boys, then they will bring home this mode of relating to people. However much they value their mother as a refuge from the masculine world, at some point they will resort to what is becoming a habitual behaviour pattern and 'take her on'. Indeed, safe in the knowledge that her love allows him to risk it, his mother is almost certainly the first person a boy will challenge.

> *Sometimes mothers allow their sons to dominate out of love. Mothers will do anything their sons tell them, not through dominance, but through love. I do everything my five-year-old tells me. (age 41)*

It is unfair to criticise such joyful subordination to a small dominant will. When he is tiny, a boy needs the confidence that occasionally beating his mum can bring. The real significance lies in whether his mother changes her approach as he matures. Once he starts school, the boy learns respect for the masculine supremacy ethos and, alongside it, develops the negative anti-feminine attitudes which are the basis for masculinity. He 'proves' his manhood by 'beating' other boys and by learning to despise everything feminine. In the interests of equality of the sexes, his mother needs to ensure she is not a 'walkover' when he comes home to test her. She must win, at least sometimes. If she romanticises the masculinity of her son and responds to his attempts to dominate with the amused or loving submission of traditional 'femininity', she inadvertently confirms what her boy is learning about females in the playground: they are lesser.

Too many people suffer because of traditional masculinity, including mothers. The testimony of men who were sons in the 1950s revealed how maternal ignorance of what masculinity entailed helped to damage the relationship between mothers and sons. While so many of the boys longed for demonstrative, emotional nurturing, their mothers were fashioning their behaviour towards them from assumptions about the 'innately' tough, self-reliant, unemotional nature of males which had no need, indeed, disliked demonstrations of affection. The view dies hard in women as well as men. Younger mothers still act from these gender stereotypes. They expect and are delighted to find evidence of 'masculine' characteristics. The discovery that their boys can also display 'feminine' qualities such as sensitivity and emotion is a big surprise.

> *My baby's only eighteen months. He's got a very, very strong personality. I don't know whether it's just his personality, or because he's a boy. He's very strong-minded about things. I admire that in a man . . . He's very definitely a boy. I hope I'll be able to keep up with him when I'm a bit older. Recently I've had to learn to be a bit firmer with my son because of his strong personality. But he's also very sensitive, which surprises me. My concept of boys being tougher [people] doesn't seem to go with him. If either of us smack him or get cross, he really cries and is hurt. (age 35)*

Despite the evidence of the affectionate male babies they cuddle, many mothers genuinely believe that, by adolescence, boys have a lesser need for emotional nurturing. They are unaware of the masculine pressures which are influencing their son's behaviour.

> *The relationship is different to a daughter because boys don't have the same needs. A boy gets more indifferent and independent as he gets older. I don't think they stop needing advice and reassurance, but they don't require the same closeness—the difference is due to male and female needs . . . (age 40)*

It is sobering to set this traditional female opinion against the sad memories—and the blame—of sons who look back from middle age and cannot believe that their mothers loved them. They recall the lack of demonstrative affection or of maternal comfort when they felt 'timid' or 'frightened'. The emotional needs they describe as being unfulfilled are no different from those a mother might expect to find in a daughter. A chasm existed between the sons' actual feelings and what their mothers presumed they felt. The women were rearing their boys according to the traditional wisdom about masculinity. They were not in a position to query its requirements even if they had perceived the need, but a younger generation of mothers can do both—if it chooses.

Women sense their ignorance of their son's world, recognise

the uncertainty it produces, but do not fully realise how it rebounds on their relationship with him, causing lasting, usually unexpressed pain to both parties and bewilderment to the mother. Unlike her son, who will clamp down his ambivalent feelings under a rationalised notion of what is appropriately masculine, the mother will be left wondering (on the unacknowledged edge of her consciousness) what went wrong between the cuddly toddler and the remote man who can barely conceal his impatience with her. At best, she will detect a loving son's strained tolerance and feel diminished by it. In her ignorance and, as generations of women before her had done, she will probably resort to the comforting conclusion that this is the 'natural' order of men.

6 Masculine and feminine

Developing masculinity separates mothers and sons far more acutely than sexual difference and women widen the gap by making stereotyped assumptions about the nature of masculinity. They expect their boys will be 'typical men'; they want them to be 'typically masculine'. In response, they shape their own behaviour along 'typically feminine' lines. Since romantic traditions of masculine and feminine involve a 'dominant' male and 'submissive' female, mothers who react this way encourage inequality between the sexes. Furthermore, in settling for the role of audience to a hero, many also pass up an opportunity to stretch their boys to emotional maturity.

A mother in her thirties reported that it was her eleven-year-old son's 'typical' male interests and male behaviour which regularly reminded her that he was of the opposite sex. She listed the elements which made her most conscious of the difference.

> *Football leaves me cold. Also, his attitude to friendship is very 'take it or leave it' and that's different to a female's I think. Lack of attention to his surroundings [is another difference], but I think I was like that when I was young so, maybe, it is not gender related. His interest in cars as status symbols also baffles me.*

Adolescence emphasises the difference further. Mothers observe the changes in height and muscular growth with fascination, swap stories with one another about breaking voices, or the first sign of whiskers, and enquire curiously of other mothers whether *their* sons are taking out girls yet, but it is increasing masculinity rather than physical change which affects them most directly. They are well prepared for the growth of independence—in some cases, over-ready for it. A mixture of preconceptions about masculinity and Freudian warnings that mothers should 'keep their distance' causes many of them virtually to abdicate authority as their boy enters his teens. Even self-confident women, whose general behaviour does not substantially alter, are still predisposed to stand back very early in adolescence and let boys make their own way. As their sons exhibit more obvious 'manly' characteristics, some mothers experience a real loss of confidence in their ability to cope. Depending on personal dynamics, they may react with feigned feminine helplessness or with the genuine abnegation of victims to a stronger will. Haircuts, homework and domestic chores might cause disagreement, but conflict between mothers and sons during the teen years was most likely to be triggered by the 'clash' of masculine and feminine.

The difficulties of adolescence vary from family to family. Among the contributions to this book, issues of over-protectiveness or interference arose for individuals but generally, the greater the emphasis on distinct male–female roles, the harder it was for mother and son to remain on good terms. Too often, the charming masculinity and attractive femininity of so many women's imaginations were replaced by dominant male and subordinate depressed female: a scenario which had sometimes been established by domestic violence from the boy's father. The lower a woman's self-esteem, the more fragile the boy's masculine bravado, the more aggressive the confrontation was likely to become. Lack of mutual interests and disparity in size and strength could become glaringly obvious to a mother, as one woman sadly discovered with her fourteen-year-old son.

> *I think mothers are easier on boys . . . because they can be intimidated by them and, like me, find their behaviour to be so totally alien to anything they've experienced as women. (age 41)*

The degree of alienation that mothers experience can be mild or very intense. At its most extreme a boy's mother may be repelled as well as confused by the change from the delightful small boy she once knew into a 'macho' stranger. In this uneasy environment doctrinaire feminism can provoke as many arguments as exaggerated femininity, which one mother demonstrated when she described how teenage pressures collided with her feminist theories. Masculine–feminine differences of opinion expanded from aggravation into full-blown conflict, each party holding stubbornly to narrow gender attitudes which the feminist element did nothing to soften.

> *I am very conscious of his belonging to the 'other' sex. He values 'male' qualities and eschews 'female' ones of caring and nurturing. He refers to the Arsenal Club and its followers as 'we' and talks about male achievements on the sportsfield a lot. I don't listen! He dresses in black and likes his leather jacket because, 'It makes me*

look hard'. He listens to 'masculine' music—punk, heavy metal, and turns off ballads if I play them. (mother 42, son 18)

Despite their best efforts, many mothers were forced to accommodate sexist behaviour in the boys they had reared. Most who commented on this explained it away as 'a temporary phase' or 'immaturity', just a hangover from adolescence. Or they found other terms to describe it. 'Rather arrogant', 'sometimes patronising', 'not slow to tell me where I'm wrong'. A frequent explanation was 'like his father'. This did not make sense at all to divorced mothers whose children had had no contact with their fathers since infancy but it was often preferable to recognising sexism. Only one mother bluntly called her son a chauvinist and wondered how it had happened. Others avoided the feminist terminology, but were equally bewildered.

My son is not a person to show feelings easily and regards me as eccentric to try and discuss these with him. (His stepfather's influence?) We do discuss (and argue about) beliefs and attitudes and other people's feelings and rights. I find him intolerant at times, but feel this is probably the arrogance of youth and the 'ivory tower university student' syndrome. He is equally dismissive of his mistakes and triumphs as though it is not 'macho' to show too much. This disappoints me but, again, time may change it. His triumphs are usually announced in a roundabout way by phone, especially for the benefit of me and his stepfather, but some reading between the lines is required to know what reaction he wants from us. He makes me very proud regularly and I tell him so. He needs to hear this, but would never admit it. (mother 39, son 19)

The shock of the different wanes as the boy matures and both parties adapt either by accepting a permanent gulf between them, or by discovering new common ground. Thankful to have survived the notorious teenage years, mothers believe that they have arrived at the final, mature shape of their adult relationship with only the arrival of a daughter-in-law likely to change it in any significant way. But, surreptitiously, masculinity continues to take hold of a mother's son. As their lives increasingly separate, some women become aware for the first time of other subtle masculine elements in their much-loved boy's character, which they did not notice developing while he was in their care. Having tried hard to teach him to appreciate others' feelings, they grope for ways to describe a mystifying development. They express it in prosaic, everyday terms, 'lacking in awareness', 'not particularly concerned with other people', 'a little off-hand' or take a specifically female perspective and call it 'lack of guilt'. They are, in fact, describing the self-focus and disregard of others which author John Stoltenberg called 'lack of ethical accountability': that distinctive male characteristic which is so vastly different to the empathetic conscience of women. One young man was well into his twenties before this trait became obvious to his mother.

> *While Andrew and I are alike in many ways, there is that difference which I feel is always there between male and female. One of the big differences between men and women in my opinion, is that men* never *feel guilty about things. Women seem always to be feeling guilty about something they said, or did, or didn't do, or didn't say etc. I don't think I've ever heard a man use that phrase. The idea is foreign to them, even the most sensitive of males! (mother 50, son 27)*

Masculine socialisation, rather than male sexuality, reinforced the difference for another mother as well. The trigger was different and she expressed it differently, but the cause was the same.

> *Oh yes, of course I am conscious of my son being the other sex. Men can switch off more than we do and don't have jobs waiting all the time! (mother 52, son 28)*

Developing masculinity does not always cause alienation and conflict. On the contrary, it can bring a new dimension to the relationship between mothers and sons which the women find exciting. Many are so delighted by the evidence of their son's transformation into a man that they begin to respond to him more as a female than as a mother. A daughter is experienced by her mother as an individual first and a 'feminine' person second, but a son's masculinity—real or potential—sometimes takes precedence in his mother's mind. Her image of how a man is, or what he should be, can outweigh his individual qualities and affect how she behaves towards him.

Psychologist Toby Green had observed the way in which a mother's consciousness of her son's masculinity could affect her reaction to him.

> I do think women tend to respond to their sons as males rather than just people. I think a lot of mothers stereotype their sons and behave accordingly. You can see a friend you thought you knew really well and, then, her child walks into the room and you hear her speak to him in a voice that you didn't even know she owned.[34]

Feminism created the need to re-think masculinity as surely as it sought to re-define femininity, but the anti-man aspect prevented the very analysis required. It forced many women to quarantine masculinity in their minds and mentally isolate it from the effects of feminism. They had to adopt one approach when functioning as individual people and another when interacting with the males in their own lives. The result is a conundrum which puzzles so many observers: a fully-fledged career woman who can be seen relating to men—or to her son—with the helplessness of stereotyped femininity. Downplaying her achievements, acting dumb; 'obliging', but never 'demanding'.

Modern mothers may have avoided analysing masculinity in the wider context, but they know what appeals to them at a personal level.

> *I guess my son's got the qualities I really wanted in a man for myself—a kind of feminine intuition, the ability to really connect with you on a spiritual level . . .*

Their feelings play as distinct a part in shaping their sons' style as did their counterparts' attitudes in previous generations when they tried to raise their sons in line with the prevailing masculine model of the 1950s. Today, it is a personal rather than a community standard which mothers aspire to for their sons. Any notions of equality which they hold take second place to what they find attractive in a man.

> *Personally, I can't stand wimpy men, so I stamp out any wimpish behaviour. I like a man to be the dominant partner, the one who is*

a comfort because, in any situation, he is in charge. Because of that, I encourage masterful behaviour. (age 37)

The desire to have a truly 'male' son could be much less specifically focused. For some mothers, it was an amorphous, undefined concept, a kind of yearning reflection of women's general notions about masculinity (including their romantic image of what 'real' men actually were). These mothers assumed that traditional masculine traits were innate and expected that stereotyped masculine qualities—such as self-discipline, dominance, leadership, self-reliance, ambition and high energy—would materialise almost magically in their boys, along with the development of a suitably 'macho' demeanour. Essentially, these mothers took masculinity at face value. There was no perception that strong, 'masculine' men could be masking uncertainty or emotional isolation, nor that the desirable qualities designated 'masculine' could be generated in women, given an upbringing that encouraged them.

One mother who held very traditional views about gender qualities appeared to expect that the onset of masculinity would automatically conjure up the decisiveness and purpose she found lacking in her sons.

I don't think about the sex difference very much. I mean I love men and I love the boys to be masculine, or male, I love that. In some ways neither of them are quite overtly male. They're not out playing sport. They're not boozing or womanising. They're not doing any of that typical stuff. They're unusual lads, but they're both strong in their masculinity . . . I like the maleness of them . . . I value it as an integral part of them. I see the extreme feminists becoming just like the men they're deriding . . . I just think they don't know how to do the feminine right, so they have to be anti-man. I'm a feminist in that I love a lot of equality. I do not see women as inferior for one minute, but I do love to enjoy being a woman and the man to enjoy being a man. I like them to enjoy their sexuality and, if you can enjoy your sexuality and feel equal in it—I don't know whether feminism comes into it. I just automatically encouraged the boys to be as male as they liked. But they're very sensitive—I haven't had to try and make them more sensitive and modern and all that stuff. I'd probably like them to be a bit more masculine . . . If they could bring up the masculine side a bit, they might get the discipline and structure and their life might come into form a bit. So, while they are masculine, I don't think they're using that side of it enough. (age 46)

Most mothers of sons derive immense enjoyment from the interplay of their femininity with their boy's masculinity: few perceive how it contradicts their goal of equality. In the name of femininity, which can also disguise a lack of self-esteem, some mothers seek 'heroes', reacting submissively, perhaps flirtatiously, encouraging masterful, even dominant behaviour. Many cede the initiative in the relationship to their son, allowing him to decide the degree of affection shown or whether to 'approve' of their actions. Their expectations are traditionally feminine. They seek love and attention, from someone they themselves can admire. A school teacher's acute eye detected the consequences of such stereotyped expectations. He watched how excessive 'femininity' governed the behaviour which mothers adopted towards their sons and the way they sought reciprocal masculinity from their boys. These were modern mothers, whose sons were largely under twelve. Just to watch them made him angry.

They overlook the fabulous qualities in their own child because they're looking for the stereotype. And they're looking for the compliments that all those other mothers with fabulous macho sons are getting. Mothers of boys with qualities of being 'the new male', the sensitive male, even make excuses why their sons don't appear to be like everybody else. I don't think a mother's really quite sure why her son's different. She still loves him, but I think some mothers have a lot of secret yearning to be, well, to latch on to the hero thing. They all want their sons to be heroes. Supreme beings. They've got to start realising that whether a boy's ten foot tall, or ultra macho, or likes listening to Mozart, he's still an individual. They can't expect him to go out and do everything in life, try to even things up for them . . . a lot of women still want their sons to be exactly like the traditional son . . . the macho, secure husband type. They're very suspicious of any other woman who happens to come near their son and suggest 'There's a whole new theory . . .'.

Yearning for heroes has implications for equality between mothers and their sons because romantic tradition provides a rationale for women to subordinate themselves. 'Adapting to lovers' rather than remaining their true selves is an old pattern of female behaviour, almost second nature. When seeking to please a man, a woman's tactic is usually what Gloria Steinem described as a unique ability 'to play down who she is and play up who he wants her to be'.[35] Asked directly if they act like this with their sons, most mothers would deny it, but the true picture can be glimpsed when they contrast how they relate to their daughters. Woman after woman confessed that she 'shared more of herself' with her daughter. Some even termed the relationship 'more equal'. In other words, she presented herself as she was, not some rosy image. Daughters were shown the unadorned woman with all her weaknesses and strengths, fears and hopes. This did not mean that her relationship with her son was deceitful, but it meant that she would play up the way she wanted him to see her. As in a true romance, a son was shown the 'best' side, the most attractive, most pleasant aspects of his mother. To a large extent, he was presented with the image rather than the reality, not the image of a lover, but the image of a perfect confidante: of woman as kindred spirit.

Older women mostly hid their true selves within the role of 'the good mother'. Among their middle-aged daughters, the picture had greater variation, perhaps including work, or study, or special interests, and always, of course, the personal version of 'good motherhood' which often concealed the strain of living up to it. The romantic aura was the same in all versions. More often than not, it was expressed as a 'presentation' similar to the way women 'present' themselves to adult men and it acted as a barrier to a young male's understanding of women. The unreality—and the inequality of this behaviour—was usually explained as 'different interests' or by emphasising daughters' 'same sex'. Mothers appear to lack confidence, as women often seem to do with adult men, that their sons will like the people that they truly are.

> *I love my daughter in quite a different way. She and I try not to dodge around issues which affect both of us . . . It just seems to take longer to work out with a girl. (mother 42, son 20)*

> *The footing with the girls is more equal. The issues to be resolved with them are more complicated and the passage more 'bitchy' and*

difficult. We have now reached a more equal sharing of thoughts and feelings, but my son, who is older, still feels the need to put things on a parent–child basis i.e. 'I won't do that because you're not going to tell me what to do etc.'. The girls seem all but past that (with occasional lapses!). I think this is probably a two-way street when I consider it. I share more of myself with the girls and they reciprocate. (mother 39, son 20, daughters 18)

I find that I share a whole lot more with my daughters than with my sons. I suppose, being women, we have such a lot in common and our interests are similar. I relish their successes which they so happily share with me. They are exuberant and outgoing and uninhibited . . . They play hard and work hard and like to share their lives, both the good and the not so good, with me. (divorced mother 49, sons 27 and 22, daughters 25 and 23)

Contrast these views with the following description of the relationship with a son, in this case an adult son of thirty-two.

I believe he is well aware of his mistakes and misjudgments, so it's no good mulling over those. His triumphs I share with him gladly. (age 58)

This is mother as her son's audience, offering praise or congratulations or admiration as required, reflecting back to him a hero image as women have done for men over centuries. No harm done? A charming custom? The boy suffers from a lack of validation for the person he really is, adding another uncertainty to the facades generated by masculinity. And the repercussions are felt by another woman who finds it hard to live with a hero's need for unstinting and uncritical admiration.

My husband was told so often by his mother that he was so clever and wonderful, that he really believes that he does not make mistakes. (age 52)

One man, married for the second time, had analysed the different attitudes of wife and mother and was quite comfortable, even amused about it. He was unaware how few of his own sex differentiate between the two female responses, how many expect the two women to be identical, nor how bitterly wives resent having to be the ones to 'puncture the self-illusion'. And what a trigger to marital conflict it can be.

My mother can be a great source of emotional comfort because she is demanding while still being appreciative, especially as she sees me only at good times so 'her baby' can appear faultless. There is no need for me to perform in order to gain her praise. My wife, of course, cannot be expected to have such an unblinkered view as she has to live with me 'warts and all' . . . Sometimes, however, it is necessary for someone to puncture the self-illusion: wives can be much better at that than mothers. (age 44)

Mothers' expectations of their children are affected by romantic attitudes. The corollary to playing up who he wants her to be and playing down her reality lies at the heart of women's failure to hold male people responsible. By extension, they play up who *he* wants to be and play down, or overlook, who he really is. If this romantic approach conceals a severe lack of self-esteem, it increases the likelihood that a boy will not be called to account.

I think, sometimes, if you can, you skate by [an argument] and ignore it . . . yes . . . I can think of a few circumstances when I've done that. Your power is not sufficient. (mother age 43, sons in their twenties)

A mother's authority can be consciously abandoned in the name of love. A woman in her late thirties, who admitted that her son was 'the light of her life', described the effect of the overwhelming emotion she felt for him. Helpless with love, and a prey to guilt, she could deny him nothing. And discovering he could always depend on her to make his life easier, he developed the habit of not taking responsibility for himself.

My son will seek my advice on some things, but generally now follows his own path. If he seeks guidance, it is generally because he chooses not to tackle something and knows I will fill in the gaps as his mum, who can't bear to let him down and would feel guilty if she did. He freely admits that I am a pushover if he wants help. . . . both his past and present girlfriend keep him organised, tidy up after him, look after him etc. He seems to have a talent for getting people to 'do' for him as his mother did in the past. (mother 39, son 20)

Sharing themselves with their girls was usually an indication of how mothers were also prepared to share general problems and responsibilities with them. They felt free to be emotionally 'unsparing' with their daughters, yet as much as possible strove to protect their sons from emotional, financial or other problems. It was the difference of a relationship between two equals and one between adult and child. In addition, they held their daughters responsible to a degree undreamed-of with their sons. With hindsight, one middle-aged woman could articulate the difference in her own upbringing. 'My brother had a much easier time than I did and was protected from all the pain and sadness which I had to share.' (age 46)

Answers from more than fifty teenage girls who participated in this project revealed that they perceived a qualitative difference between their relationship with their mother and their brother's relationship with her. Many recognised the boy's relationship as different and sometimes called it 'special'—one girl describing her brother lovingly, but succinctly, as 'Mum's plum'. Few had any complaints about favouritism towards the boy, but many contrasted his 'jokey' relationship with their mother with their own 'more responsible' one. Neither boys nor men drew any similar comparisons, but some were envious of their sister's relationship with their mother and it was not just jealousy at being excluded by an obvious gender alliance. They appeared to detect the greater frankness and, in a sense, the greater trust, but could not articulate what they were missing.

How can motherhood combat centuries of tradition which celebrates the romance of masculine and feminine interaction above all others? Few mothers would even want to try. For many, it is the essence of everything they treasure in the mother–son relationship. But allowing romantic stereotypes to shape the relationship can misinterpret the boy's real nature. It also reinforces cultural assumptions that women enjoy subordination to dominant men, which is particularly detrimental when a difficult realignment of male–female relationships is taking place. More personal are the implications for a son's adult life—and for his mother's. In the long and, for the mother, potentially lonely years, her romance can rebound. When someone else takes priority in his affections, he may find it easier to let go the relationship with his mother. Let her go. To keep the peace. There is no victory for her either way. If she wins, her son loses. It is the strongest argument of any for eschewing romance and developing the capacity to relate as two independent—and comfortably interdependent—people.

There is another factor which causes mothers—and adult women—to 'spare' the males they love. Even when they do not understand masculine conditioning, they recognise its fragile nature—and make allowances. Women's role in helping men preserve masculinity, often at the cost of their own subservience, begins out of a mother's love for a vulnerable child. The recognition of the uncertainty behind the posturing, the inarticulate relationship with other males, including the father, is part of the heartache of mothering a boy. It is also the glory and the romance which makes a man's mother feel she is special in his life. It is a fundamental cause of the conventions of masculine and feminine behaviour. It will not change so long as proscriptive masculinity creates so many men in need of reassurance.

There is an unfortunate consequence. In settling for a reassuring role rather than adopting the same unsparing approach they take with daughters, mothers pass up a unique opportunity to help their boys reach a greater depth of emotional maturity with its potential for more insight and psychological flexibility. They comfort the boys but in the process hinder the development of self-awareness. Psychologist June de Vaus defined emotional maturity as:

> . . . the ability to consider the experiences of others in deciding on our own actions and also the ability to accurately interpret the behaviour of others.[36]

Empathy, in other words. Sometimes, just consideration. By this definition, how many adult men are emotionally mature? And how can they be expected to achieve that state given the way masculine conditioning develops self-focus, limiting the capacity, or interest, in interpreting others. In recent years, many women have tried to help sons imagine how other people feel, but they contradict their own efforts if they simultaneously 'play up' how he wants to appear at the expense of what Stoltenberg called 'ethical accountability', or if they only share his triumphs and overlook his shortcomings. Imagining how others feel is ineffective, and nearly impossible, unless it is accompanied by self-awareness.

Mothers sense masculinity's fragile nature and try to shield it from a too confronting reality: 'I'm more worried that my male child will get hurt emotionally than my female child'. The result is either emotional dependency on women or its alternative, isolation. A man who wants to take emotional responsibility for himself rarely has the tools to do it. Deprived of communication skills and unfamiliar with the emotional ruthlessness required for mature awareness, he barricades himself behind a facade of self-sufficiency, which increasingly becomes impenetrable.

By colluding to preserve traditional masculinity in these ways, women risk something else of great importance to their own happiness. Assumptions that allowances must be made for men, but not for other women, divides the 'weaker' sex among themselves. Too often, women will sacrifice their relationships with each other rather than hold men responsible. Their unequal expectations can hurt their female friendships. They can damage their relationships with their daughters and their daughters-in-law. One woman saw the effect, if not the dangers.

> *Boys are the opposite of girls so, from birth, we are dealing with the opposite sex. If our girlfriends treated us the way our boyfriends did, we would probably never forgive the girlfriend. Yet, how many times do we forgive the boyfriends? So it is with our male child. They have us around their little fingers from the moment we set eyes on them. (age 40)*

Much affectionate tolerance has always existed for a mildly romantic interaction between a parent and child of the opposite sex. So long as it observes appropriate boundaries, it can be charming, intriguing, inspirational, reassuring—and enjoyable. Mothers vary in the degree to which they recognise their own devotion and the lengths to which it can take them, but other women watching from the sidelines see it clearly. The good-natured amusement of the past was expressed by 72-year-old Betty.

I know the girls can hoodwink Dad, the same way that boys can with Mum. I noticed this when teaching at mixed-sex schools, how the girls often manipulated the young men teachers and the boys did the same to the young women. So I guess it is a way of life.

Even some fathers could be among the indulgent observers, one man suggesting that his wife's relationship with his son reminded him of his mother.

The few mothers who articulated the overwhelming love they experienced for their son gave various reasons for the emotional helplessness it created. Louise believed that the fact that she was single and only a teenager when she gave birth to him made her feelings more intense. A subsequent marriage and the birth of two daughters had not diluted her passion.

Many times, during my life with my kids, I have felt that my son was the 'light of my life'—something never to be seen by the girls, I hope. I suspect they have felt this though (and resented it). Whether my reaction to him was because of my situation, or just overwhelming maternal love in lieu of other relationships, I'm not sure. Probably a combination of both. My daughters call their brother 'spoilt'. He acknowledges he can manipulate me if he wants something . . . However, as the kids finished school, I have tended to take my life back . . . I have created more of a distance between myself and my son in recent times by withdrawing a bit. But, whatever happens, the love I have for my kids is unconditional and my greatest achievement. (mother 39, son 20)

In general, the gender expectations, the assumptions and the romance which shape mothers' approach to their sons does not appear to have changed over recent generations. Mothers, some of them avowed supporters of equality between the sexes, still succumb foremost to their sons' masculinity, displaying a 'typical' feminine submission to a delightful but dominant force. Rachael was thirty years behind Betty's amused tolerance. She was a liberated, self-aware woman, yet her parental authority could be displaced instantly by her son's male attraction—and she gave the same reason as Betty.

. . . one day I was annoyed with him about something and when I started to reprimand him, he came over and lifted me up, put me

over his shoulder and carried me around the house. Needless to say, this reduced me to laughter. I believe that sons are able to charm their mothers in much the same way as daughters charm their fathers. (age 40)

The significant difference is that mothers have been, and generally still are, the predominant parent, the one in a position to encourage their child's self-awareness, to hold him responsible for his actions—or let him avoid them.

In its most positive form, the sexual difference adds an enjoyable spice to the interaction between mother and son. Through it mothers validate their sons' attraction for the opposite sex—and gain much personal enjoyment in the process. But the suggestion that they flirt with their sons is too dangerous for most women to contemplate. Like the sons, their first instinct is to deny it. Except for a few—mothers with enough self-esteem to feel confident in their mothering and in the parent–child relationship, were not afraid to assert *Vive la difference!* One woman whose description of her parental role was confident and unstereotyped, had no qualms in detailing how much she revelled in her sons' distinctly masculine presence.

When I go out with my daughter, I feel sorry for her *because she is so beautiful and I am not, but we do have fun together. And I love to go shopping with my boys. They are so tall and straight and walk just behind me like a bodyguard. (It's even better when my husband joins us.) They make me feel feminine and pretty. This is probably the place to say also that they are very affectionate. They will hug and kiss me very readily. I suppose I flirt with them a bit, but then, I do with their papa. (mother 48, sons twenties)*

Whether the sex difference has been over-emphasised as a complication in the mother–son relationship is a subject for further research. Analysing the perceptions of the range of men and women interviewed in this study—nothing extraordinary about them, neither case studies nor examples of exotic neuroses—tends to reduce the role of sexuality and highlight the impact of gender stereotypes. The masculine–feminine interaction shapes the style and tone and quality of the relationship. It highlights different interests and differences of opinion. It can emphasise equality or inferiority. It can be a source of enormous pleasure or intense aggravation and the intensity of the patterns revealed here suggest that further research should now give as much emphasis to the impact of gender expectations and behaviour in the mother–son relationship as they have long done to the effect of sexual difference.

7 Kindred spirits

In their oblivious masculine fashion, sons are usually unaware of the star role that they play in their mothers' lives. It is but one element in their developing self-focus and so the attention feels natural rather than special, most particularly natural when it is bestowed by women. For the same reason, they are unlikely to give it much thought, let alone analysis. They may be aware of their mother's ministrations, but unconscious as to the nature of it: whether it expresses a mild appreciation of difference or slavish devotion or romantic flirtation.

Sisters notice every small nuance in the relationship. Among adult women, the sight of their mother placing their brother on a pedestal—endowing him with romance, or power, or status—fills them with emotions ranging from angry scorn to alienation and hurt. If they ever accepted the discrimination as girls, feminist insight changed their attitudes and, in maturity, they are neither oblivious nor tolerant. Today's teenage daughters regard their brothers with amused tolerance, but their mothers' generation has forgotten what that indulgence feels like and judge their brothers and their mothers harshly. Observing closely from the sidelines, by middle age these women have intimate knowledge of both parties and this combines with female empathy to produce some sharp, if not always disinterested observations. They see clearly how their mother abandons the role of parent with their brothers and this difference is resented even more if she continues to take an authoritative stance with them. Watching their mothers relate to their brothers as males rather than sons, they are often the first to detect the detrimental effect on the man's adult relationships. In her mid-forties, one sister found an ally in her brother's girlfriend. Together they breached the pattern of the man's relationship with his mother, drawing attention to dynamics which he had never noticed.

My mother has a great need to be demonstrative with my brother. She's quite coy and girlish. She talks about him constantly—'David took me here . . . David and I did this . . .'—almost like a lover. . . . [My brother] recognises it more now that my father is dead. And because his girlfriend and I have helped him see it.

After twenty-five years of feminist influence, some men have become more acute at detecting a pattern similar to the one described so bitterly above. Even so, they usually have to be triggered into awareness by a woman. One man who had been alerted by his wife could see the truth of her criticism. He felt burdened as well as treasured by his mother's loving attention as he struggled to rationalise the tension it created in his marriage.

> *My wife used to feel my mother was 'flirting' with me sometimes before we became parents. Since we've had a child, she hasn't noticed it. Perhaps my son gets a lot of the attention that my mother used to give me. I certainly didn't recognise my mother's affection as flirting, but must admit I did perceive a touch of competition from my mother towards my wife in the early days. My wife has noticed how Mum refuses to let me lift a finger whenever we visit my parents—I honestly have to fight her for the tea towel and I'm always served first at meal-times. I don't believe I got things any easier than my sister—we both did very little around the house—but my wife feels I am my mother's favourite child, although I don't notice it. My mother does refer to me as her 'first born' occasionally and I'm sure that is the reason behind her favouritism, if any. How much the relationship is affected by the fact we're the opposite sex is a very interesting question . . . I've always got on with, and communicated better with women than men, but communication is not a strong point between my mother and I. (age 42)*

Men found nothing appealing in the idea that they can beguile their mothers. The suggestion was so unwelcome to most of the older sons that they rejected it out of hand, denying any suggestion that the old cliche about 'winding their mother round their little finger' might apply to them. They dismiss this as manipulative behaviour and not something they would choose to do. Only one middle-aged man admitted to the possibility that he had taken advantage of his mother's love, but the example he quoted was not one women would agree was fair to him. The issue was too serious. And it occurred before there was acceptance that men could effectively care for children. His widowed mother's decision to abandon her independent life to care for his children, was behaviour which other women would probably describe as justifiable maternal sacrifice, in the circumstances. With hindsight he can see the sacrifice but, in taking her help for granted when it occurred, her son was 'typical' of his generation.

I probably could wind my mother round my little finger. It wasn't a thing I abused. Well, I might have abused it round the edges. But I don't think I (seriously) took advantage of it. My current partner says I could have used her if I'd wanted to, but I haven't . . . I'm not a user of people. If anything, it's the other way round. I probably used my mother in ways I would now think beyond reason, particularly the period when she looked after my kids for two years until I remarried. If I had that time again, I wouldn't have allowed her to do it. I would have done it all myself to the best of my ability. At the time, I didn't understand her thoroughly. It's only been looking back and talking with my sister and, occasionally, with my aunt, that I've understood where she was and how she acted and why she came to the position she was in. And I've come to understand my own past better. (age 53)

A much younger man came closer to what women mean when they characterise a mother and son by saying that the boy can wind his mother round his little finger: he recognised the persuasive edge he held on his mother. A bystander might have suggested he could 'charm' her, but he insisted the effect was trivial.

I probably can wind my mother round my little finger. Not in a major way, but over little things. I can probably convince her to come round to my way of thinking. She'd probably be more resistant to my sisters. But only marginally. (age 28)

The youngest group of sons understood more exactly what the question meant. They were less defensive, more relaxed with the idea and their responses were often hilarious as well as informative. The brief chronological quotes set out below inadvertently, but vividly reveal the changing flavour of the relationship as a son matures.

It's practically impossible to wind her round my little finger. (age 10)

There's absolutely no way *that I could 'wrap my mother round my little finger'. (She's a bit too big!) (age 12)*

Sometimes I can. (age 14)

I don't know about wrapping her around my little finger but, for the softer touch, it was always Mum that I went looking for. (age 17)

No, I can't wind my mother round my little finger. She can always see when she is being manipulated and will only allow it to go as far as she wants it to. (age 19)

I wouldn't say I can wind my Mum around my little finger, but I am quite persuasive. *(age 19)*

I do know my Mother very well, but I cannot wind her round my little finger! Perish the thought! Seriously though, my Mum knows when I am trying to get my little way with her and then usually jokes and catches me out.(age 20)

I would say I can wind my mother round my little finger, sometimes. When she is determined that she's mad at me, there's nothing I can do. Although it is easier these days. (age 21)

It is always a question of perspective—and of course degree. Even in extreme cases, where women might see a son's power over his mother, men are likely to interpret the behaviour quite differently. The opposite point of view was illuminated in the brief answer of a thirty-year-old man.

What I like best about my mother is the way she makes me feel the most important person in the world to her. If I want my Mum to do something for me, she usually does it without argument. It doesn't feel that she's 'wound' around my finger, but that she wants to do it for me.

One son did recognise the extent of his power. Aged only twenty-one, he had the delicacy to appreciate that it meant he must never take advantage.

I almost feel I could make her do anything I wanted for me but, knowing that she would, I wouldn't like to abuse it, for fear of losing it.

A similar generational difference was revealed when the sons were asked directly about their mother's influence as a woman. The older men's first instinct was to deny their mothers any influence at all, a predictable reaction and yet another unhappy consequence of the intense and narrow masculine socialisation with which most of them were reared. One middle-aged man was uncompromisingly and devastatingly blunt. Dismissing his mother's influence, he went straight to the core of his feelings about her.

I have never considered the fact that my mother is a woman has had anything to do with our relationship. Certainly, if it had, I perhaps should be a woman-hater, or a serial killer! (age 42)

Any suggestion that they might flirt with their mothers was certainly not welcome to most men in the older group.

I don't think . . . well, there is certainly a jokey relationship and lot of affection between my mother and myself. But I'm not aware of the sexual thing as I am with a number of women with whom I have totally platonic relationships. We have a strong intellectual (link) . . . we've both got a love of language and books and history and a strong sense of family . . . If you saw us together, you might think that spark is there, but it's not something I'm aware of. There's a lot of game-playing between us. I think what I've been describing in our relationship is unique to us. It's not like my sister and mother. I'm talking about gentle affection, teasing. It's not exclusive to my relationship with my mother. It's just got those particular elements because we share this passion for literature. (age 47)

Another son from the same generation had a very similar relationship with his mother but, perhaps because she was long dead, he was one of the few who did not feel threatened by a suggestion that he had flirted with her. He was even prepared to identify a definite sexual element in their interacton. Confidently describing the part it played, he realised with surprise, half-way through his answer, that competition with his father had been a contributing factor too.

It is possible to be sexually drawn to your mother. I can remember as a small boy about eight years old, being very attracted to her. I'm looking back as an adult, of course. I can remember a certain attraction of a semi-sexual nature. But at that age, she was an attractive person. There was a flirtatious element (between us) from time to time—in conversation and joking . . . or was there . . . interesting. I was dodging my father's possessiveness and I think that made me wary of a similar sort of connection with my mother. She wasn't possessive. She never made me feel her apron-strings. My father had those . . . they were everywhere. . . . My mother was concerned, warm, but I never felt she was trying to tie me down. I wasn't trying to antagonise my father, not consciously. I think probably that happened as I got older. She and I would have a joke about something. We had a sense of humour which bounced off each other. . . . From the age of about twenty-one there would have been a bit of gentle flirting, very light, nice, fun, but, yes, I think I would have been conscious that my father was feeling a bit out of it. (age 50)

A few of the older men were prepared to acknowledge the role of what one called 'the crossover effect', referring to the way in which mothers tended to favour sons and fathers to favour daughters. One man in particular emphasised this as the reason that there was less tension between himself and his mother than in his relationship with his father. 'There was more liking and less antagonism.'

A much older man in his seventies described another era when conventions of masculine and feminine behaviour were clearly defined and part of the pattern of daily life. They flavoured his relationship with each parent quite distinctly, emphasising difference which, at its best, as in this case, was courtly and pleasant.

It made me more helpful and gentle to her. And attentive. For example, if she was carrying a basket in the street, I would immediately offer to carry it even as a small boy, but (I knew) Dad was much bigger and stronger than me so he could carry his suitcase himself. Because she was a woman I also felt I could confess mistakes more readily. She would laugh! Dad was more likely to be anxious and correct me.

But conventional manners and respectful gestures could be totally misleading. Sometimes they disguised a son's angry ambivalence. One middle-aged man declared resentfully that, regardless of how he felt about his mother, the fact that she was the opposite sex nevertheless meant she received 'ingrained attitudes of chivalry and undue respect'.

This bitter echo from a childhood of forty years ago was rarely duplicated by the children of the last twenty-five years. Among the contributors to this book, the noticeable generational shift continued in the emotional quality of the relationship between sons and their mothers. Some of the older women might unduly sentimentalise their boys and, certainly, there were a number to whom their sons were nothing short of heroes, but for them it was more often from an emotional, as well as a physical distance. In that generation, the vast gulf between male and female perception and experience was often very obvious. At their most confident, however, older women felt that they had achieved a relationship which was lovingly empathetic although perhaps distant in modern terms.

> *Some mothers I know have intimate knowledge of all their sons' friends in adult life, as well as all minute and intimate details of their day-to-day life. This I do not know, nor do I have a great desire for it. So, in this sense, many may say that I do not know him. Yet, if understanding his moods, likes, dislikes, hurts and joys, is knowing, then I truly know my sons. I know their strengths and failings and love them for, and in spite, of them. Colin is the middle son, for whom I have a strong bond. Perhaps because I almost died when he was born, or because I see myself in him. (age 73)*

Some of the younger mothers, whose sons were entering their twenties, made startling claims to a level of emotional intimacy which resembled the most romantic female ideal of a kindred spirit. As one ventured ecstatically 'He knows me through and through . . . to the very core'. Another, as was often the case, identified with the son as a male version of herself: '. . . he is the most like me. We have some kind of indefinable rapport'. Aware that she was laying herself open to scorn, one mother confessed, bravely but hesitantly, that she believed that there was a psychic bond between herself and her son and described an incident which illustrated the uncanny, inexplicable links that can develop between human beings who are emotionally close. Not every women exalted such an intimate bond, one describing the whole idea of knowing her son 'through and through' as 'a bit off'.

In the main, the sons agreed with their mother's claim that they knew them 'through and through'. About half were convinced that they understood her better than their father did. But the generational change was again apparent in the emotional quality of their response. While most sons, both over and under thirty-five years of age, agreed that they did know their mothers very well, such agreement from the older men was rarely complimentary. 'Predictable' was the description which recurred in their answers. They knew her 'through and through' because she was so 'predictable'. Only one man from this generation saw his knowledge as a special intimacy to be treasured.

> *We have a degree of understanding that my father appears incapable of with anybody except another soldier . . . Perhaps because of the time we spent together in my childhood and the way we shared my development as a person, we not only understand, but have actually come to think alike. My father does not understand my mother and appears to believe her rarely-expressed dissatisfaction is unimportant. (age 44)*

Most of this man's peers rejected the possibility that their mother might understand them. Few, however, were quite as adamant as the following:

> *My mother thought she knew me, but she never knew anything about me. Nor what I really thought a lot of the time. I simply didn't tell her. I'm not saying that I know her 'through and through'. I wouldn't know how she actually felt, but I could predict what she would do and how she would react to any given situation . . . There were things my father would do that I knew would displease her [but] he didn't know . . . I think it was just an aberration on my father's part because her own brothers would know. It wasn't that I knew my mother better . . . my father just knew her worse. (age 46)*

The attitude of the younger sons was quite different. They showed little sign of discomfort in admitting their closeness to their mothers and their replies indicated that many did indeed feel an empathetic link similar to the claims made by so many women. Like the older men, however, a significant number expressed astonishment at how little their fathers understood their mothers and some were scornful that the adult men could be so oblivious to feelings which they felt were plain. Divorce was not the explanation for this discrepancy. These were sons who either grew up in, or who were still in, two-parent families.

> *I'm not sure how well I know my mother. What I am sure is that my father has no idea of what makes her tick. (son 34)*

> *I think, in certain respects, I do know her better than my father. I am always surprised that, after more than twenty years, he will still do things, unintentionally, that I can see plainly will hurt her or cause rows. (son 20)*

The joy and the sorrow, the close bonds and the distance which a mother can experience with her child of the opposite sex were summarised most eloquently by a woman in her mid-forties whose son had recently left home.

> *I'm very conscious my son is the 'other sex'. That's 99 per cent of the pleasure in the relationship, surely. I'm extremely aware that a man's path is still different to a woman's and I have to help him cope with this and not expose him too much to a woman's viewpoint. By that I mean that I don't want to 'convert' him to the woman's lifeview. They are different paths, experiences and pleasures. We can share them to a certain extent, but not totally. Are mothers easier on boys than girls? Possibly. My brother had a much easier time than I did and was protected from all the pain and sadness which I had to share. I* think *there is a very different relationship between mothers and sons. They hold the key to each other's being/ego/better self for a long time. This can be precious, poignant and magical. It could be lethal and destructive. It may be that the existence of this relationship makes mothers go more easily on sons. (age 45)*

Sons confirmed the special relationship with their mothers and the younger generation, particularly, valued its role in their lives without reservation. But they did not celebrate the mother–son bond at the expense of their fathers and made it plain that a balance between both parents was what they wanted. Although acknowledging that they felt closer to their mothers, virtually all of the sons interviewed blamed their inadequate relationship with their father on his physical absence. Among the older sons, this was usually given as a simple, clear-cut cause and effect and they did not analyse it further. Any disappointment, disillusionment or regret they might have felt was buried so deep that it might never have existed.

> *I am much closer to my mother than my father and gave up years ago wondering why. It does not bother me one bit, and it's not spoken about much. My whole family know that feelings between Dad and myself could be better. Nobody knows why this is the case. It may be because I always sided with Mum when they used to argue, and argue they did. I will never forgive my father for the arguments he caused, many over nothing. (age 37)*

Younger sons showed much greater emotion. They still cared. Most began by desperately wanting to be close to both parents and tried hard to keep a balance even when the odds were against it because, as one twelve-year-old reluctantly rationalised, he only saw his father late at night or at the weekends. 'Now, I think I am slightly closer to my Mum, but very slightly.' Most of the younger generation did not maintain the fiction of 'absence' to explain their problems with their fathers. As they entered their teens, they increasingly summarised the difficulty under another heading: 'communication'—and they meant the style of communication, not the substance. Although a number revealed that they had interests in common with their mothers, like literature or music, the reason most sons gave for their better relationship with their mothers was the women's greater capacity to listen and remain non-judgmental which they contrasted unfavourably with the defensive, rigid attitudes of their fathers. During adolescence the latter could result in a complete breakdown in the relationship between man and boy. All too clearly, the boys saw the communication limits which were imposed by their fathers' more judgmental, dogmatic personalities. Sadly, it was always assumed to be a personal deficiency rather than a cultural problem. The male generation of the 1940s and 1950s, who judged their mothers with little regard for context, are now being judged by their sons. The following is a fair expression of the general consensus:

> *I greatly enjoy my mother's company. She is a very good conversationalist and as we share the same interests, in particular literature, there is always a great deal to discuss. She knows a great deal and I value her opinion. She is much easier to talk to than*

my father, who tends to defend his opinions dogmatically, taking any dispute as a personal slight. (age 19)

Another young man, at barely twenty years, was mourning the loss of a relationship with his father, which he had valued. The eldest of four children, he took no comfort from his lopsided closeness to his mother and tried hard to explain the deterioration of the bond with his father.

It's as though this question has been personally written for me. I would say that, presently, I am closer to my mother than my father. Firstly, I do not see my Dad as much as my Mum and, secondly, Mum is always readily available at home. This is not by choice though—I hate the way I get on better with my Mum than my Dad—I want them both to be equal. I want to be close to both. My Dad was closely involved in my early years, up to when I was about 14, then I lost his respect and trust by not working at school and other such misdemeanours. After that age, we never seemed to be as close as I remember when I was younger . . . My mum has been a peacemaker between us when we did not get on and was always concerned with our relationship. I think my Dad would like to be more involved, but cannot manage with the time/work etc. . . . and with four children, it's hard to divide time evenly.

Overall, a majority of sons from all ages declared that they were closer to their mothers. Many of the older men, who were now fathers themselves, described the pattern continuing in the present generation, most saying that their own sons were closer to their wives. They unanimously maintained that the difference was due to the greater amount of time their wives spent with the children, but the pattern in the contributions gathered here suggests instead that it is a consequence of the poor quality of father–son interaction.

The difficulties however, are not all one-sided. Masculinity takes over from empathy when sons relate to their fathers. They can be as dogmatic and defensive as the older men, each generation making the other worse. Even on trivial matters they refuse to give ground. One young man in his late twenties was a demonstrably reasonable and flexible thinker when dealing with his mother and when thinking through issues intellectually, but his relationship with his father, although harmonious, was straight out of the 'masculine' textbook. Self-aware in other ways, he had no idea how their mutual masculinity limited their ability to relate. Having mentioned how his father's simpler, 'black and white' attitudes made him prefer his mother's company, he then described a classic masculine stand-off with each party refusing to be beaten by conceding that the other's idea might have merit.

> *My father is . . . less complicated . . . tends to think more in black and white . . . my mother is quite intelligent and capable of talking with anyone on any matter . . . Even now, I'd rather do something with my mother than with my father. I'd rather be alone and doing something with her because I understand her. The competitiveness with my father, now, that's a Pandora's box. It's not a conscious thing but I can think of lots of times when it came out in me as a young lad . . . He would have an idea . . . and I'd have an idea—and each of us would insist we were right and wouldn't give in. (age 28)*

Sons soon learn to rely on their mothers to act as conduits to their fathers. Women condemn men's emotional cowardice but they help perpetuate it by mediating between father and son. Their assumption that they must be the people to do the 'emotional housework' is never more evident than when acting as peacemaker, messenger and interpreter between their partner and son. Masculine conditioning is the primary villain which damages men's ability to communicate, but they learn as boys that their mother will fill the gap for them. She will talk to their father on their behalf. Naturally, as adults, they look to their wives to do similar emotional tasks. If mothers more often said: 'Ask your Dad', rather than 'I'll speak to him', perhaps father and son would learn to communicate better, but women will not risk it until men relax masculine defensiveness so that children—particularly male children—can get a receptive hearing. Some women were pleased that their boys used them in this way, believing it was a sign of their special status in their children's lives. Others were puzzled. They regarded themselves as the strict disciplinarian and their husbands as 'soft': the boys' refusal to ask their fathers directly did not make sense.

Mothers' work in breaking the news, easing the way, facilitating the emotions, continues into adulthood. Men are reluctant to admit it happens and a son's perspective sounds very different to a mother's, but it is recognisable because it is the popularly accepted description of such scenes. It is a clear demonstration of how society glorifies the mother–son bond when it should be weeping for the fathers and sons who cannot talk to one another.

> *Whenever I ring home, it's always Mum I speak to and she fills me in on what Dad's doing. Occasionally, my father answers the phone and we have a bit of a chat and he'll say, 'Oh well, I'll get your Mum'. It's not . . . I'm still quite friendly with my father, but he knows the strongest relationship is between myself and my mother . . . When I left for college, my father drove me to the station, Mum wasn't there, and he said: 'You should really keep close contact with your Mum because she has this special relationship with you. She'd be hurt if you didn't keep in touch with her'. Does he feel displaced? . . . My father would be a kind enough man not to, well not openly resent it, but he can accept it because he's got a special relationship with his daughter. (age 26)*

Women begin with an idealistic concept of their son's relationship with his father. It is romantically integral to a woman's deepest motivation for having children by the man she loves: 'giving' him sons. Watching man and boy find companionship together is an extension of that emotion. When, as too often happens, the bond is displaced by antagonism, many find consolation in the greater emphasis of their own relationship with the boy.

Analysing the mother–son bond, examining every small component, concluding all too often that some of its most celebrated ingredients are not necessarily in the best interests of either party, is not intended to deny its value. Despite some justifiable carping, the reality remains that the tie between a woman and her son can attain some peculiar level of awareness not duplicated by any other relationship between the sexes.

Even sons who resent it recognise the unique bond with their mothers but they are at a loss to explain its qualities. Although usually failing to analyse its nature, women have no doubt that its source is empathy, that emotional skill on which they place such emphasis that the scathing label 'empathy junkies' is not always entirely misplaced. Often wrongly termed 'intuition', women's capacity for imagining the feelings of others—empathising—is notorious to the point of intrusion. It is the basis of the emotional facility which they use constantly in their relationships with the opposite sex of all ages and which mothers take for granted when relating to their sons. One woman described the essential role female empathy plays when faced with impenetrable masculine conditioning.

> *Doug was always very bright . . . [but] I remember his Junior School headmistress telling me she 'wished he would be naughty sometimes'. His father had taught him to 'keep a stiff upper lip' and this has certainly affected him. He does not often express his feelings, even though* as his mother, I can often read his thoughts. *(age 51)*

Perhaps empathy is the clue to explaining the unique quality of the mother–son bond, the point at which reality and legend meet. If researchers are correct in claiming that masculinity progressively closes down men's capacity for empathy, then it follows that the only woman who will ever know a particular man while he is still empathetic, is his mother. By the time he has matured enough to marry, masculine conditioning is likely to have reduced, if not eliminated, his ability to relate to his partner with empathy. Is this why a boy can 'read' his mother, when a husband cannot? Is this why some women treat their sons as precious beyond anyone or anything else? Are they the only males who can offer women the emotional intimacy for which so many yearn? One intelligent and perceptive 23-year-old found the words to describe his side of this special link.

> *I do feel that I know my mother better than anyone else who loves her. I doubt that I know her, to use the cliche given, 'through and through', but I am sure that I have spent more time with her in an emotionally open state (if you understand what I mean) than anyone else, perhaps even her parents. It sounds a little arrogant to claim this, but I am relatively confident that it is true and that she would agree.*

8 The balance of power

Women begin their role as mothers from a position of power, yet many end up subordinate to their children. Their failure to balance power if the child is male is not just a personal disaster: it also lays the basis for inequality between the sexes in later life. But women cannot win. When the reverse occurs and the mother dominates her son, she is so mocked and derided by the male culture that this, too, demeans and subordinates women generally by providing the source of some of the most infamous maternal images in Western society.

Several elements can create an imbalance. The dictates of masculinity is one. Women's own feelings about how femininity should respond to masculinity is another. Just as significant are the deeply buried triggers in a mother's psyche. Psychologist June de Vaus emphasised in her work *Mothers Growing Up* how being a mother gives a woman the initiative to control the distribution of power because she is often the only person who understands the child's needs as well as her own.

> Because she is responsible for both sets of needs she holds the balance of power in her hands. Some women find this extremely difficult. But the mother's ability to balance her needs with those of her child is critical for the development of the relationship.[37]

De Vaus argued that if mothers had difficulty achieving an appropriate balance of power, it was due to ways of relating which they had learned in childhood. She challenged the feminist argument that all inadequacies in mothering arose from the oppression of women into the maternal role. She recognised how the pressure to be appropriately feminine and/or the aspiration to be a 'good' mother could contribute to women's mothering difficulties, but she maintained that maternal behaviour—which is often assumed to result from full-time motherhood—could actually be created by childhood anxieties.

> Motherhood is often criticised on the grounds that mothers are frequently dominated by children. But helplessness in mothers is one of the symptoms of failure to balance power with the child. Mothers suffering from anxieties over conflict and disapproval cannot argue for their own needs . . . It is impossible to argue

> logically that society insists on women's powerlessness by making them mothers when motherhood itself demands the healthy use of power. Women develop powerlessness in relationships as a result of interpersonal experiences which are not necessarily associated with femininity.[38]

According to de Vaus, learned anxiety is fundamental to women's expectations of relationships. She asserted that the key to mothers' understanding their relationships with their children, is first recognising the anxieties which influence their own behaviour. Contrary to popular wisdom, anxiety about her own performance, not her children's, can cause a woman to love conditionally. Their achievements reassure her. Fear that she is unloveable creates a mother whose doubts can only be allayed by her children's obedience and for whom the solution is to control their lives tightly. Another model is a mother who self-effaces herself, acting constantly as though her needs are unimportant. Very likely, she learned that this behaviour will avoid the conflict which makes her anxious.

De Vaus found that the most common anxiety pattern among mothers was the need to avoid conflict. It was a habit which they had developed to cope with relationships during their own childhoods. Consequently, some women were chronically unable to make any demands for themselves, displaying the very behaviour which is popularly applauded as 'feminine' or even 'good' mothering. Stripping away these attractive stereotypes, however, reveals that they are presenting themselves and their needs as unimportant. De Vaus took feminists to task for blaming this subordinate behaviour completely on women's limitation to the 'feminine' role of mother. Instead, she contended that the loss of identity which feminists blamed on motherhood arose from the woman's personal anxieties—such as fear of conflict—which were neither unique to motherhood nor to women.

> . . . identity loss can be the result of ways women have learned to deal with conflict and insecurity. Motherhood does not necessarily produce such symptoms. Even more interesting, unimportant mothers today still generally behave in a more stereotypically feminine way as a consequence of their fears. This indicates that

> the choice to be rigidly feminine may mask other choices which are equally destructive for women.[39]

Given that so many women consciously and deliberately commit to traditional notions of 'femininity' however, and given that the examples de Vaus quotes in her book are predominantly problems between 'unimportant' mothers and their male children, it may well be that the answer lies somewhere between the two. Whatever the cause of this 'hidden' personal anxiety, a distorted balance of power between parent and child is the result.

Most modern women want to achieve equality between the sexes but, even when they understand that there are wider implications if they let their sons dominate, not all can necessarily alter their behaviour. One woman described how she could not overcome her instinctive yielding to a male person. Reared in a tradition of submissive femininity, she found it enormously difficult to hold her ground in an argument, particularly against a male. It was a classic example of the problem in separating learned anxieties from feminine conditioning.

> *I have seen very intelligent women being treated as slaves by both small and large children. I include girls because, to be fair, I have seen female children treat their mother like 'shit', but my reactions are different. When a mother allows a male child to behave in a selfish, bossy, demanding manner, I cringe at the thought of another male chauvinist pig, but, if it is a girl, I just register that the world is in for another horrible self-centred person. Humanity is lessened in both cases, but with the boy we have the added problem that women are worse off . . . My mother's reaction to men was to boost their egos and pretend to be dumber. When I was in my twenties and quite political, she told me I had better be careful or I would 'lose my femininity' . . . I have always felt that I had to change or adapt to my lovers, not the other way round. I don't think I do that with my son—although if he gets really angry, I will back off completely. (age 40)*

The elements which cause mothers to cede power to their children intermingle. Those which disadvantage women are the most insidiously disguised. Romantic ideas about male–female relationships can make maternal subordination appear to be a delightfully natural result of the sex difference. Equally misleading are compliments about being 'typically feminine' or a 'good mother'. They hide the self-effacement which, in reality, is too often lack of self-esteem. In other words, the ways in which women are disadvantaged in the balance of power are hidden by many assumptions. Distortions which disadvantage the child—and particularly the male child—are not masked in this way. They attract severe criticism. The most notorious distortion of power between mother and son is the version sons have made famous, the only one in which the mother remains in control, by dominating her son's entire life. This mother is Phillip Wylie's 'mom'. It is also the only relationship in which sons are seen to lose. Not surprisingly in a society ordered by the male point of view, it is the only one which publicly castigates mothers for their 'failure'. Some of these deceptive assumptions have been exposed through women's increasing confidence in asserting their point of view.

The reverse is also true. Masculinity predisposes men to accept heavy responsibilities for the 'weaker' sex which can advantage women. In the past, a mother would turn to her boy without hesitation or guilt if her marriage broke down, or if she was suddenly widowed. It was simply part of the burden women placed on men—placed on sons, particularly eldest sons. And it was a load men expected to carry, many accepting it without complaint. Although rarely capable of offering their mothers emotional comfort, they often made enormous financial or career sacrifices to take care of her. The nature of the mother–son relationship might have been different then—more emotionally remote, perhaps—but the practical responsibility for a mother's welfare was no less real or heavy. A mother in her sixties described the lifelong commitment which her son had made to her welfare. Despite all her praise, it did not occur to her that the sacrifice could have been more equally distributed.

> *My son was overseas when my husband walked out on us, left the farm which we had hoped to buy one day. I had not been allowed to tell our son of the disintegration of the marriage before he left and he really had no inkling of it. This is what raised him to hero status in my eyes and what I will never forget: even though he was*

having a wonderful time and had intended to stay overseas much longer—he came back when I needed him most. He helped me carry on the farm by changing his promising career. He studied to become a teacher, trying to combine the job with saving for a life on the land. Eight years later, when the farm was for sale, he and his wife sold their house in a comfortable country town and bought half the farm so I could continue the life I love. Now he has three little ones and I am still working hard, hoping he will not sell out when I cannot work any longer . . . He has a healthy respect for his wife and is often caught 'betwixt and between', but generally things work out.

Mothers in similar circumstances today feel less entitled to burden their sons. More of them have the skills and the confidence to take care of themselves and they resist calling on adult children, particularly in middle age. Many are also very conscious of the emotional danger in leaning on their children. Therapists, counsellors, psychologists and other professionals in the area of marital breakdown have accumulated an enormous depth of knowledge about the implications of such a breakdown for children. Aware of the temptation to turn to children to fill the gap left by a partner, family court counsellor Jill Burritt was typical of her profession in urging divorced parents to take care.

Don't let yourself need the children too much . . . You can very easily fall into the trap of seeking emotional support from your child . . . They need you to be supporting them more than ever. They don't need to be looking after you.[40]

Despite greater awareness of the risk, children can still get caught in a distorted reversal of the power relationship with their mother where she turns into their child. One counseller found a teenage boy silently bearing an immense emotional and practical load following his parents' divorce.

There was one boy, about sixteen or seventeen, who wasn't doing very well at school . . . I discovered his mother was in and out of a psychiatric institution and he was carrying the burden of the world on his shoulders. He obviously cared about his mother. He was doing the shopping, the housework etc. It's amazing what some boys go through without anyone having any idea. He was most caring, kind and wonderful. There was nothing to be done. He was glad he could talk about it, share it with someone . . . His father had remarried and was living a nice, normal life. He seemed to have no appreciation of what his son was going through. The father had zero emotional feeling and the boy was quite sensitive. He was just doing what he could. He didn't blame the father, even though he was pressuring his son to do well at school and the boy was failing.

Psychologists have long identified the danger of parents who lean on their children but, in recent decades, the growing number of sole parent mothers has made it a topic of urgent debate, much being stimulated by traditional ideas concerning the importance of a male role model for sons. After initial alarm as the divorce rate climbed, research increasingly suggests that this kind of emotional dependency is no more likely in single mother families than in those with two parents.[41]

Many women would certainly claim that they can be just as emotionally needy within a marriage as alone and that over-dependence on their children, particularly their sons, is less likely to occur in the testing, self-aware, self-defined environment of a family unit which is under their sole leadership. A man in his fifties confirmed that it does not require divorce for mothers to lean on their sons.

As my parent's marriage was less than happy and communication between them was a major casuality, I became mother's confidante because father did not assume that vital role. (age 52)

A much younger man in his twenties had a similar childhood experience.

From an early age, I took on the 'man of the house' role as my father was away a lot. After they had arguments, I would put my arms round her and comfort her.

For many women, divorce is a liberation and an opportunity. Alone at last, they structure their families in a way that suits them. A predominant characteristic of the single mothers who contributed to this project was their determination to run things in a democratic rather than authoritarian manner. Far from leaning on their children, they established an interaction deliberately based on equality and mutual responsibility. They shared power. Expressed in many ways and with different degrees of urgency, this egalitarian aim recurred frequently in what they had to say about life on their own. One mother, as they all left Britain following the separation from her husband told her boys explicitly how it would be.

> *On the plane back to Australia, I declared that we were all starting a new life and we were helping each other. I was determined that we would be a democratic family and that the boys should feel that they could tell me everything. It was going to be tough and it was, but I had help from my father. (mother 48, sons 20 and 18)*

A number of sons had experienced divorce, or some other trauma, which changed their relationship with their mother. Few of them were bitter or resentful and those who were had been caught not so much by their mother's demands but by what they saw as their father's disregard for the vacuum he left behind when he initiated the divorce. They felt obliged to fill the gap by supporting their shocked, distressed mothers. When the women initiated the separation, the effect on their sons was quite different. With hindsight, the young men valued any extra responsibility which had been given to them and spoke positively of the effect on their personal maturity or the benefits of a different type of family life.

> *When I was thirteen my father died and this changed my relationship with my mother. She took on the role of both parents while, at the same time, I was required to accept more responsibility. (age 20)*

> *The relationship with my mother has changed over the years, especially since my parents split up when I was 13. Being the eldest, I was given more responsibility and I was forced to mature much quicker. This split was good and the change in the relationship was good for my own personal development. (age 18)*

> *When my parents' marriage fell apart, we were all pretty much incorporated into the negotiation of how we were being reared. My mother never treated me when I was young, or a teenager, as though there was any subject I wouldn't understand, or anything that couldn't be discussed. (age 24)*

When Dad first became ill, we all grew up in a big hurry, my younger brother most of all as he had to look after the farm . . . I think Mum looked more to me for support and reassurance simply because I was the eldest and because I am an easy person to talk to. I try to listen. In a crisis, you do develop a lot quicker than otherwise. I know that I learned to accept situations and started to deal with them rather than try to avoid them. And I like being able to talk with Mum as an adult and share family things. It is as comfortable in some ways as being a protected child again. What is awkward is looking at Mum as a person and a woman with flaws and failings. You notice some as a teenager, but not in perspective. Now, I understand more things which puzzled me as a youngster and why my parents are the way they are. (age 28)

After years at boarding school since the age of ten, I felt increasingly distant from my parents . . . When I was twenty-one my father left my mother to live with another woman and my mother tried to kill herself. I was away at university at the time and, unknown to him, I had decided to leave home. His desertion radically changed the situation. I felt quite close to my mother during the subsequent traumas . . . I admire her for rebuilding her life after my father left. Not only did she form many new friendships and took part in new activities, she also became more open-minded and independent. . . . I did not see my father in the ten years between the divorce and when he died. (younger son, 40)

The older generation of women accepted men's authority as natural. Contemporary mothers feel quite differently. Divorce made some of them very conscious, even threatened, by the possibility that their son might exert male power in the same way as his father. Usually they tried to defeat it at the source, resisting behaviour or attitudes similar to those they disliked in the older man. Some directly criticised personal characteristics which were alike. Others, unable to stop themselves, reacted to their son just as they always reacted to their husband, triggering the boy into behaving as his father had done. Together, mother and son re-played not the romance, but the arguments and the battle for power between husband and wife.

I don't want him to be like his father. He can manipulate like his father, although he's coming to terms with that and dropping it. His father's a very manipulative man—in retrospect, it was very like my mother's manipulations . . . When my son and I have arguments [now] I guess either side provokes them. But my son provoked them for a long time, because he discovered the power of remarks like his father's. Remarks that could put you on a stage, wind you up and get you going. And the more dramatic you got, the more he enjoyed it . . . He learnt the power from his father because that was something my husband used to do. (mother 50, son 26)

A man in his fifties, whose parents divorced twenty years ago, experienced the full force of his mother's resentment because he was like his father. Their relationship had never been warm and he left home early, returning after a long gap around the time his parent's marriage broke down. An eldest son, he was possibly more like his father in manner and behaviour than he realised. Newly liberated from the male hierarchy of the army, he may even have tried to lay down the law. Certainly he could provoke his mother without even trying.

Mum and Dad divorced about three years after my return from Vietnam . . . My mother and I had a huge argument over it all and Mum told me to get out of her life. By this time, I had realised that I was as strong as Mum and, looking back, I think it was a clash of wills. This is not to say that I was not also at fault. We finally made up two years ago and, so long as I follow the party line, things run smoothly. Should I disagree at all, the comment is likely to be: 'You are just like your father'. (age 52)

The battle for equality between women and their adult partners has inevitably spilled over into some mother–son relationships. Divorced only a few years, the mother of a nineteen-year-old boy confessed that her son sometimes felt both the impact of her bitter anger towards his father and against the wider male culture too.

I think some of my resentment towards his father, and to the male ego generally, has coloured my attitudes to Paul, usually when we're having a huge row. I can, for instance, recall shrieking at him, 'You're a boy and you'll grow up into a horrible man*'. Yet, conversely, by fair means or foul, he managed to get his own way more often than the girls. (age 47)*

In a particularly damaging example of parental backlash, a

mother's antipathy towards her ex-husband caused her to bitterly reject any resemblance in her young son. The nine-year-old boy's struggle to establish his identity was constantly jeopardised by his mother's distress about his likeness to his father. She was a corporate executive who was used to directing her own life. When she could not control how her son developed, she became angry and frustrated. The boy's teacher was a helpless bystander who could do little but offer sympathy.

> *Everytime he visited his father, he'd come back with his traits and that's what she didn't like. She couldn't cope with any signs of his father. I'd get letters which reflected* her *emotional state, not the child's. He'd come to school with his eyes all puffy. I'd ask, 'Did you have a heavy morning?'. And he'd say, 'Oh yes, I had another fight with Mum'. They were constantly locked in conflict. He wanted to assert his identity and his mother wouldn't let him. She dealt with him on a high emotional level. Used adult mechanisms to talk to a child who hadn't reached that level yet. He matured reasonably quickly after that, rejected his mother a lot earlier than the rest of his class'.*

Divorce or death can create an upheaval which changes the existing relationship between mother and son, either resulting in dependency or sparking a tug-of-war for control which may not have occurred otherwise. Whatever the cause and whatever the exact dynamics, a prolonged power struggle between mother and son leaves a dreadful legacy, even for a boy who ultimately breaks away from his mother's control.

A young man interpreted his life as one long battle with his mother. In his twenties, he was still trying to resolve its legacy of confusion and uncertainty, only just beginning to trust his own judgment and to shrug off an identity which had been imposed upon him, rather than allowed to evolve from within. The relationship with his mother had felt to him like a constant power struggle.

> *My mother always thinks she's right, all the time. Sometimes I think she's trying to make me look bad, so she can look good . . . I definitely felt that she didn't want me to be ahead of her . . . or she didn't think I could be . . . I wanted to be more equal . . . I couldn't get it. I still feel I'm not really able to get it. It bugs me . . . I don't know whether she's interested in my ideas. I think she's*

more interested in her own . . . It gets a bit competitive, you know . . . a bit silly. (age 24)

Different eras have offered different explanations about why some women fail to distribute power appropriately. Earlier in the century, and in the post-war decades, the weight of opinion followed Freud and blamed mothers entirely for impeding the separation process from their children. Subsequently, the feminists of the 1960s blamed patriarchal society for oppressing women into motherhood and forcing them to seek power through their sons. Influenced by modern feminism, psychoanalysts then altered their theories and joined feminists in advocating greater involvement by fathers. No one denies that some mothers retained a detrimental amount of power over their sons but, intent on universal theories and universal solutions, neither group has given much weight to mothers as individual women with individual and very personal histories. Increasingly, therapists and counsellors now look for the core of a woman's mothering difficulties in her own background.

Domination by the mother is the most legendary distortion of power between mother and son. Sons do not see a woman's inherent weakness, only her power. In an attempt to defeat her, they have mocked and derided this type of mother for generations but, contrary to popular assumption, mothers 'control' neither because they feel powerful nor because they want to dominate. Nor do they necessarily seek control to compensate for their powerlessness in other areas. June de Vaus insisted that it is fear that drives mothers to excessive control—a corroding anxiety learned in their childhood. They are frightened of their own inadequacy in a threatening world and believe their 'failure' can only be avoided if they stay in control. 'Their principal symptom is panic. Their principal strategy for survival is total control'.[42]

The most unobtrusive form of maternal control, at least to the lay person, is guilt. Acording to Dr John Buttsworth, who worked as a psychiatrist for many years, it is also the most difficult to treat.

I've seen numerous patients, aged anywhere between their twenties and fifties, who live with their mothers. They're impossible to help because the reason they live with her is a mixture of many elements. Basically, they're living with their mother because the love they got was conditional. They were loved providing they would give love to their mother. So, to actually separate from their mother makes them feel not only guilt, but unloved. They think they won't be loved any more if they leave. That's why they're so hard to help. You can say, 'It's time you grew up, time you left'. But they feel, 'I won't be loved anymore'. They stay with her to keep the feeling of being loved alive.[43]

Guilt, wielded by mothers, is so powerful that it can even defeat masculinity. Despite the urging of other men, a son caught in the web of conditional love stubbornly sticks by his mother. He is almost certainly additionally burdened by gender notions of his masculine responsibility towards the feminine person who is his mother—and by ideas of how a 'good' son should behave. Psychologist Toby Green agreed with John Buttsworth about the difficulty of helping a son who is controlled by his mother in this way.

Boys have this thing about being a 'nice guy'. About the way nice guys should behave. Their mother instills that in them and they buy it. In order to break out, they would have to feel like they were a real bastard. When a mother hands over the responsibility for her well-being to her son, it is one of the most severe problems. The hardest to cure. Worse than any other combination. Mothers and daughters aren't as bad as mothers and sons. A mother behaves like that for various reasons. Maybe her relationship with her husband isn't working. Or perhaps being her son's mother defines who she is.[44]

The son whose mother defines herself by his existence bears a heavy burden. Her idea of 'a good *man*' can be as constricting as the maternal tentacles around a good *son*. Although not tied to his mother's life like the latter, the good man carries her notion of masculinity forward into his adult life where it makes him vulnerable to another woman. In his father's 'absence', his mother has passed on her feminine vision of the qualities which make a good man. Too often it contains the very self-effacing elements which also make up the 'good mother'. A man in his fifties detailed them to telling effect:

A strong sense of duty. A strong sense of giving to others,

> *unselfishness. If you think of yourself, it's selfish. You should never do that—a man doesn't . . . A man wouldn't cry. To be a man you had to be tough and self-sufficient . . . Men should be nice, agreeable, polite, unselfish, self-sacrificing, gentlemen. Anything else was looked on with dislike.*

A man with this maternal legacy can spend his entire life bearing the burden of other people's dependence. It can take the form of financial and physical obligation but even, perhaps particularly, includes carrying another's emotional dependence. This son does not perceive that what is demanded of him is unreasonable, any more than he understands what is being taken from him: the lack of space for his own life and respect for his person. Such men's vulnerability exposes them to a degree of emotional harrassment which amounts to an invasion of privacy. This son can never say 'No'. He can never tell anyone to leave him alone because he has neither a sense of entitlement, nor of self-preservation. His mother subverted those qualities long ago with her insistence on the unselfish qualities which made an acceptable man. She brought him up not to hurt anyone, even at cost to himself.

Female guilt plays a fundamental part in a mother's inability to balance power with her children, but mothers who use guilt to control are not power-hungry monsters, nor are they necessarily victimised by their maternal role. They are just as likely to be simply distressed individuals. Guilt is also a personal response to personal circumstances. June de Vaus made the point that there are too many variations of guilt to assign a single cause. She identified four forms of anxiety which result in particular styles of maternal behaviour and described the subtle but different kinds of guilt that each embodied: mothers who love conditionally and feel guilty because their children are not good enough and, by implication, neither are they; rejected mothers who feel guilty because they dislike their children; unimportant mothers who feel guilty if their needs create conflict; and precocious mothers who feel guilty if anything goes wrong.[45] De Vaus challenged the feminist conclusion that women feel guilty either because they have been trained to cater to the needs of others or because men make them so.

Not only is there wide variation in the cause of guilt, but a

> distinction has to be made between true guilt and false guilt . . . False guilt keeps us tied to the rules we learn about how to behave. It functions to stop us changing. True guilt occurs when we have set out to hurt others. The vast majority of maternal guilt is false guilt.[46]

Mothers do the best they can, often in difficult circumstances. Trying to rear a large family, cope with financial and emotional problems of their own, they can be unaware of the stress building up in their child until it explodes and leaves them bewildered at what went wrong.

> *. . . for years he virtually wouldn't come near me. Everything I said, he felt was controlling him, or over-mothering him. My ex-husband didn't see him much either. He was angry with both of us. And he just had it in for me. I didn't know what it was, or what I'd done, because we'd actually always got on well. But he felt threatened, I think, somehow . . . I think I probably played a typical mother and tried to tell him what to do. All that basic stuff. But I always validated him . . . I didn't see myself as being particularly pushy, or intruding into his space at all. I always felt we had a good relationship . . . At one point recently, I acknowledged him and, I think, apologised for all the misunderstandings we'd had. And he felt like I'd actually given him some power. He shifted from then on and he's become more willing to see me . . . We actually get on well, but it is just very respectful on my part. (age 49)*

Many mothers spoke about the difficulty of judging how much is too much. Knowing the depths of their own emotions, it was always 'too much mother' they feared, never 'not enough'. Like women from time immemorial, they found the balance difficult—and the restraint.

> *I'm aware I tend to over-mother and be intrusive about his thoughts and feelings. I know it's right he should grow away from me, but it's hard. (mother 42, son 6)*

> *I'm a very protective mother, overly protective physically and emotionally. My husband has taught me to let go a bit. And the children say to me 'Mum, don't be stupid . . .' It's not that I have a particular fear for any one of them. It's more a general, normal caring. My husband and I have probably had more arguments*

about my over-mothering, my over-protectiveness than anything else. Is it a misjudgment of what they're up to? No, not a misjudgment . . . I just forget that I've got to the point where I'm not totally responsible for them. I felt I had to do all the decision-making for them. (mother 44, sons 20s)

It's very difficult when you love someone so much and know them so well to stand back and watch them suffer the awful experiences which are part of growing up . . . When he was at college, our mutual love of theatre gave us a contact point and, in this hybrid atmosphere, I could be the 'over-the-top' mother I had always suppressed. (mother 46, son 20)

Not all sons are oblivious of their mother's efforts at self-restraint. The son of the mother above who had always stopped herself from going 'over-the-top', was a young man with an exceptional level of both self-awareness and empathy. Confident of his mother's love, he was unusual in realising how she had not allowed her strong feelings to burden him.

Was her love an encouragement or a burden? For a moment I was going to answer 'both', but that would not be true, because she has never let her love be a burden. When she has seen that it would weigh me down at all, she has suppressed it for my sake, and perhaps also for hers. (age 21)

Western society would be far less colourful without some of its classic portrayals of the mother–son relationship, but the dominant male viewpoint decrees what will be the community's targets and it can be cruel to mothers. It predisposes sons to interpret the women's actions negatively. At their worst, these archetypical mother–son relationships can be painful and damaging. In a mild form, they are simply the different dynamics between two people which arise as much from personality, individual experience or education as a difference in sex. Harmless or damaging? Sometimes it can be hard to tell where the borderline is crossed.

The intrusive, nosey mother is the most vulnerable to differing perceptions by male and female—or mother and son. Interference rather than an extreme need for control is the problem. In an excess of mothering, a woman sometimes fails to give her child enough space to develop in comfort. She is everywhere and into everything the child does. Sons and daughters can both suffer from this kind of maternal overkill, but it is the male experience which has made it legendary. Mother interfering in son's life is the version we see depicted so often in our culture. As a mother–son relationship pattern, it is a disastrous reality but it can also be seen simply as distortion—a victim of masculinity. Ever-conscious of the threat which 'too much mother' poses to their manhood, sons very easily label a high level of maternal concern as 'intrusion' while the same amount of involvement from a father might well be described as 'support'.

The problem is exacerbated by men's undiscriminating acceptance of the motherhood ideology. Lacking practical experience, they believe in the myth. And rather than pointing out where the perfect mother diverges from the human woman, most mothers feel obliged to emulate the idol, so sons' judgments are shaped by what they are led to believe about mothers. Like their presumption that there really is a 'typical' mother, many of the participating sons assumed that mothers, generally, were 'over-protective' but most then claimed that their own was not. Whatever the truth, many women are undoubtedly disadvantaged by masculine judgments such as those which played a role in the relationship detailed below.

Twenty-seven-year-old Robert was in a position to observe the childhood genesis of a relationship which very likely culminated in adult life with the kind of fierce animosity apparent among several middle-aged sons, including two who opened their contributions with the remark: 'The best thing about my mother is that she lives on the other side of the continent'. In telling the following story, Robert spoke kindly of a misguided woman. He was blithely unaware of the mother–son tragedy he had witnessed: a woman who had to resort to ringing her sons' friends to hear news of him, with the sorrowful nostalgia of a second-hand link to a happier past which had contained his presence.

My Mum was always supportive at school without being interfering. Some of my friends' mothers would interfere very much either directly with their children, or by ringing teachers. Mine could be concerned. And she'd speak at Parent–Teachers nights when it was appropriate or she'd do her turn on the Canteen . . .

> *What bugged me most about my mother was, what I regarded then, to be an unjustified degree of interference in my life. Too many questions. Even when you got home from school: 'How was school?' Sometimes, it was enough to drive you up the wall. That was primary school . . . As a teenager, school sort of took over. I probably had less contact with my mother. But there were a couple of lads in high school who had what we thought were extremely intrusive mothers. We didn't ever go round to their place. We'd think, Oh we're not going round there because Mike's mother asks questions all the time. And Mike would say 'Yeah, she does it to me all the time . . .' Mike's mother was always doing Canteen, or on school committees. She was always in touch with the teachers, finding out things. It got to the stage where he'd have nothing to do with his Mum. He'd say, 'I've got to get out of home. Can I come round to your place?' It made him the butt of a lot of jokes . . . His mother hasn't changed today, but we're older so we can cope more. She's just very interested in what's happening. I was home recently for my brother's wedding. She heard I was back and rang up for a chat. I didn't mind. She was just being friendly. . . . Mike is an only son, with one sister. He lives up in Edinburgh now.*

Damaging intrusion? Well-meaning maternal concern? Over-anxious blundering? And what contribution did the attitudes of the male peer group make to the relationship? Whatever the reality, it is the interpretation which has lasting impact. Seething with what will become lifelong resentment, the son struggles out from under and hastens to put as much distance as possible between himself and his mother. She will count herself lucky to hear from him once or twice a year and bury her sorrow too deep to touch. After all, it is only natural. 'He has his own life to lead'.

The male interpretation decrees that this son had a lucky, and justifiable, escape from the ultimate stereotype of motherhood. The female reality is tragically different.

9 | Victims

Masculinity makes the rules for the mother–son relationship. It dictates how both parties must think and behave towards each other and controls through the weapon of stereotypes. Superficially, the advantage may appear to be all with the male child but 'mother's boy' is a male-created image which victimises sons as surely as it hurts women. Mothers do not want to risk being seen as the typical 'mother of a son'.

Sons free themselves to agree with the general disparagement of mothers by distinguishing their own mother from the species 'mother': she is declared to be 'not typical'. Few men can imagine how the constant denigration feels to women, how it hurts and demeans underneath even while, on the surface, they bask in the exultation of motherhood as something which the male sex holds dear. If more sons could empathise with the corrosive impact on the mothers they love, the belittling remarks might diminish. But mothers themselves do not challenge the pervasive derision, most cope, presumably, by using the same mechanisms as men: they mentally and emotionally draw a distinction between themselves as individuals and themselves as mother, society's favourite target. It is possible to ignore the insults when one is the special exception. 'At the tender age of eight, my son thinks girls are pretty awful! I am the only acceptable female!'. (age 39)

Masculine ideas which keep maternal affection in check have included images which have become so much a part of everyday speech that their derogatory implications pass unnoticed. Reference to a mother's 'apron strings' was in common use when today's middle-aged sons were children. A woman, now well into her sixties, used it unselfconsciously without realising how it kept her at a distance:

> *My son and I are close, but hug or kiss very seldom. I have always endeavoured not to 'tie him to my apron strings', yet he and his small son are the most important people to me.*

'Petticoat government' was another term used for belittling maternal control and it could still be applied without comment to a mother in the 1970s.

> *He was a very intelligent boy who, according to his primary school*

principal, objected to 'petticoat government'. Unfortunately, as his father was rarely home, 'petticoat government' was the only rule.

Feminist insistence on gender neutral language arose from such unthinking disparagement and, by the 1990s, no headmaster intent on preserving his job would blatantly express such sexist sentiments. But the attitude can still be detected in the palpable male distrust with which mothers' appraisals of their boys are so often received. They are listened to, but not heard.

Forty years ago, intense peer pressure was exerted on boys to dissociate themselves from all females. The extremes to which this could go were touched on by a mother, now in her eighties, when she recalled a compliment about her eldest son. It demonstrates the constraints on boys during that era—and the dreadful humility of women.

Another delight was when a neighbour told me John always spoke to her if he met her in the street 'even if he was with other boys'. She thought this rather nice, so did I.

The atmosphere has improved considerably in the intervening years, but his peers' views still make a loyal twelve-year-old defensive in the 1990s.

Compared to other mothers, she is very *different. My friends call her an embarrassment. I would not want her to be any different because she is best the way she is.*

The miserable ambivalence this kind of peer judgment creates in a son can be imagined, but it is more than matched by the emotional blow which the developing tension in the relationship deals the mother. She is always conscious that she may burden or embarrass her son and her sensitivity is generally accurate. Another twelve-year-old could say calmly: 'She irritated me when she came to the football and no other mums were there. She knew this and left'.

During childhood, masculine peer pressure increasingly conflicts with a boy's love for his mother, driving it underground and making his tenderest feelings a secret which can be displayed only at the cost of his manhood. It is just one of many hurts that he must learn to conceal. The betrayal of a friend who deserts him to be part of the gang, or the lance of mockery from a boy he trusted, are among wounds inflicted by masculinity, but the thickest scar tissue in the adult man hides the unkindest cut he suffers in those growing years—the realisation that his love for his mother is a weakness that he must conquer. The feelings of inadequacy this process also creates in the woman concerned are usually overlooked.

One of the pivotal uncertainties for women has been when—or, more recently, whether, to kiss their sons. Traditionally, masculinity dictated that boys give it up and mothers stop it. In the 1990s, the masculine rules about when kissing is allowed have relaxed, but not very far and probably not much beyond sections of the middle class. For many people, maternal affection is still widely incompatible with developing masculinity.

Men's inability to talk about their feelings has hidden the pain this causes them. The fact that boys suffered because they were not actually touched or kissed enough, has not been publicly discussed. The men in this study, especially the older ones over thirty to whom it is a deeply hurtful issue, appear to have no idea that the male culture in general, or their own actions in particular, may have stopped their mothers kissing them. In the privacy of their consulting rooms, professional therapists are helping men, and women, to recognise the vast change in what is deemed appropriate affectionate behaviour, to accept that people of both sexes were less demonstrative thirty or forty years ago, often showing love by actions rather than words. But few query the role of masculinity in this dearth of affection. Most sons of the post-war decades had no idea that their personal struggle to live up to a particular vision of manhood might have stopped their mothers from showing them affection.

It is and always has been a great but unacknowledged sacrifice for mothers to give up kissing their sons. Most describe their delight in the physical affection of their boys, joyfully describing the love that they were free to give when the children were tiny and the way in which it was reciprocated. This reaction was as prevalent among older as it was with the younger mothers. Regardless of generation, and almost without exception, women nostalgically recalled the cuddles and hugs and kisses of their baby boys, but most revealed how they expected to lose the initiative to kiss them. In the drive to develop emotional capacity in boys, contemporary mothers have made some progress in keeping the barriers down, but they remain intimidated by the masculine mystique and do not feel sufficiently empowered to object about the way it repulses their affection, even when the children are still in primary school. Young mothers still anticipate the time when the kissing will stop. One woman in her late twenties was thinking about it even though her son was only two.

> *I am very conscious that my small, soft, cuddly, infant son will one day be bigger, stronger, taller than me. When (or if) will the cuddles/kisses end? Can I expect them from an adult son? Amazing to imagine him being as big as his father, an adult, not my baby anymore.*

Mothers start to restrain themselves when the boys go to school even if they don't fully crystallise why. In so doing, they hand the initiative for affection to the boys but, as masculinity closes in, their sons become increasingly inhibited. They begin by showing less affection for their mothers in public, a split which the mother of an eight-year-old described.

> *He likes to sit with me at night if we watch TV and he always has to have his twenty kisses at bedtime. He now doesn't like public displays of affection, but does enjoy a cuddle at home. (age 38)*

By adolescence, many have stopped either seeking or showing affection in private too. Their mothers try to understand, to laugh it off, but the masculine culture which is governing their sons' behaviour often leaves them hurt and bewildered. In the way of women, some think they have offended and search for a fault in themselves. Janice did this in the mid-1950s:

> *A significant moment I remember well, was when he was about twelve and going away to scout camp for a week. He kissed me goodbye, but that was the last kiss I got until he was about seventeen. I realise it was all part of becoming a man. At the time, I wondered what I had done to deserve his not wanting even to walk down the street with me. (age 83)*

Boys still behaved this way in the following decades. And mothers still suffered in silence as a 46-year-old mother revealed. She was describing a time during the early 1980s.

After thirteen the relationship was trickier. Hurtful when he wouldn't sit with me on the bus (behind or in front instead), or speeded up to walk away from me if boys from his school were around. I never said a word. Pretended not to notice.

It was a common tactic to conceal any pinprick of hurt by turning youthful masculine 'rejection' into an amusing family story. Answering a direct question, a son who is now approaching thirty was prodded into remembering how he once felt. While recounting the circumstances, he realised the scene had been kept alive in his mind by his mother talking about it over the years.

My mother used to walk us to the end of our street and I wouldn't walk with her when I was at primary school. I'd walk a couple of paces in front because I didn't want to be seen with my Mum. Or people to think I needed my Mum beside me. My sister was there too, but I wouldn't walk with her either. We both went to the same primary school for three years, but I wouldn't be seen with her.

Most adult sons have forgotten how they behaved as boys. Any specific instructions that they may have given their mothers have faded from their minds. But the women remember vividly. The pattern has not changed with the generations:

When Jack reached ten, he began reserving the affection he'd always shown for when we were alone . . . 'Don't kiss me or hug me in front of so and so, will you Mum?'. And, of course, I wouldn't though sometimes he would cast a warning glance just in case I forgot. (age 61)

This son is now in his late thirties but the 49-year-old mother of a young man nearly twenty years his junior obeyed the same commands even though, in this case, they were unspoken. 'He is not over demonstrative, only kissing me at home and not in public. I respect this though'. And a woman in her eighties had experienced these strictures twice in her long life.

My son was all of sixteen years when he made the profound statement: 'I'm not going to kiss you any more, Mother'.

(My youngest grandson was nine years when he gave up, so I suppose I was lucky.) I accepted this as part of growing up. It proved transitory.

Sadly, it does not prove transitory for all mothers. There are sons who stop kissing out of the need to appear masculine and never start again.

I'm not sure how it happened but, in recent years, he and I don't embrace when we meet, although we embrace our friends and my husband and I kiss regularly. (mother 51, son 29)

Fathers have no idea what is really happening either because traditional masculine assumptions frame their appraisal.

My son is fourteen . . . I suspect history is repeating itself. He and I are becoming much closer and he seems to have somewhat scant regard for his mother. It may be just a phase, but it looks familiar. She tried to run his life. (age 42)

The impact of masculinity is as much a mystery to men as it is to women. Another father watched his son rebuff his wife and, although a man of some insight in other ways, he revealed not the slightest awareness of the masculine context in which they were operating and no appreciation of the sorrow a five-year-old's decision could impose on a woman.

I've got two sons. The oldest is very independent. At the age of five he announced he wasn't going to kiss his mother any more and I don't think he ever has, or only on very rare occasions. So, I don't think there's been a very close friendship between them. In fact, he is closer to me than to her. (age 53)

Even fathers who tried to smooth the relationship between their son and their wife saw it only as a personal problem rather than a cultural one also.

Our son is seventeen. His mother feels very close to him but he's hurting her now, which she can't understand. His behaviour got so bad that I spoke to him about it . . . It was just a general style of behaviour, not particular issues. . . . He improved significantly in his attitude towards her for a while, but he's slipped back a bit now. (age 48)

A young mother today still experiences rapid loss of status when her son starts school, a loss which goes beyond the natural development of independence. Almost immediately, the boy learns to feel differently about his mother and his attitude affects her. Her feelings for him remain the same, but her self-image wavers as she begins to see herself through his eyes—an embarrassment. School brings a new uncertainty to their relationship. At first, it can be put down to the wrench of separation and the beginning of independence but, as the first week and then the first year or two slip by, the mother of a son is forced to take account of the ambiguous element in her role. Her supportiveness is struggling to survive his embarrassment. Most women abide by the masculine verdict and even those with strong self-esteem start to feel tentative. A teacher at a boys' primary school in the 1990s described a scene with which he was all too familiar.

> *By the late primary years if a mother has to come to the school for something, the boy gets embarrassed. She's usually bringing a note, or a forgotten lunch, or medicine. She peers round the door, gawking, embarrassed herself because she's in the sanctum . . . basically she's there to spy as well. The boys turn to look. A boy nearby might say 'It's your mother'. The son will walk over with his eyes down. She'll want to touch him, but he'll keep a metre apart so she'll hand over the lunch box and there'll be a pregnant pause for about ten seconds. The teacher's waiting for action. The son won't know what to do. He glances at the class, aware they're watching to see if he'll kiss her. The mother slinks off, feeling useless, and getting no feedback. Fathers rarely come. I've seen about ten in fifteen years. It's always the mother. If the father does come, he's businesslike. 'I've got my son's sweater. Could you give it to him?' I usually ask if they'd like to speak to the child. The mothers invariably say 'Yes'. The fathers say 'No, just here to deliver this' and the child's reaction to him is very laid back and businesslike too. If his mother's at the door, there's an automatic assumption of 'soppiness', of him being a baby. You can sense it. The father doesn't drag up those emotions. I'm at a co-ed school now. The boys seem to have a more relaxed attitude to their mothers coming here . . . I think women are less alien because there are girls in the class.*

The net effect of masculinity on the mothers of boys is to erode their self-esteem. A mother, whose son was barely two years old, noticed how many of her peers lacked confidence.

> *As a general observation, I do think mothers are easier on boys. I have been at many playgroups where mothers assume that they are not qualified to handle boys and obviously leave it to their husbands to deal with them later on.*

Perhaps lack of confidence is an explanation for mothers' infamous 'easier' treatment of boys. Perhaps, like this mother of a nineteen-year-old boy, they doubt their own judgment about how to handle them.

> *We decided to send him to his father's old school believing it to be best because I wasn't quite sure what to do with him as he approached his teens.*

Mothers' expectations of the relationship with their sons becomes progressively humble through primary school, adolescence and into adult life. An elderly widow who was on good terms with her adult son mentioned how much she would like him to escort her to the theatre occasionally. She never asked him, not because she feared he would refuse—on the contrary, she had sufficient confidence in their relationship to believe that he would agree to take her—but because she was concerned that her presence might harm his reputation. 'I thought he may not enjoy being known as a man who goes about with his mother.' (age 73) Once again, there was continuity down the generations. A woman twenty years younger reacted with the same humility when her son invited her to go out. 'I was unable to go but I felt very pleased he considered me worthwhile material to be with.' (age 53)

There is a name for what these women dread. 'Mummy's boy' is a tag men fear. It frightens women too. Wielded persistently as one of the most effective weapons for herding men into masculinity, it also keeps mothers in line.

> *I have consciously tried not to be the heavily involved, devoted mother of an unmarried son . . . (age 54)*

> *. . . I think I always held back a bit with my son—all those fears of mother's boys (the Italians call it mamismo,) of incest, of not wanting him to be a sissy . . . (age 43, son 14)*

What do women fear? The typical image of the 'mummy' as in 'mummy's boy', is a woman so possessive that she is oblivious to the damage she is doing to her son. Her style may range from frankly dominating to manipulatively feminine, but she is also oblivious of how she herself appears to onlookers. Just the fear of seeming to be this particular kind of 'mummy' often governs women's behaviour, including those who are actually most sensible. They fear 'her' for their own sake, for the effect on their sons and, even if realising that they actually bear no resemblance to this stereotype, they fear that something they do may make their boys perceive them that way.

Men fear being called 'mummy's boys' because it questions their manhood. Male opinion of mothers who act like 'mummys' can appear quite tolerant because it is just an extension of the general disparagement, but the 'boy' is everything they do not want to become and they despise him without compassion. Fear of a 'mummy's boy' tag makes men reluctant to discuss their mothers. They shy away, frightened that they will seem unmasculine by showing interest in the relationship. Not surprisingly, given the harsher masculine climate in which they were reared, it was the older men who were most conscious of this danger.

I'm doing this because it's interesting, but it shouldn't be taken out of proportion. It represents one small fraction of my life which is very important to me. The great bulk of my time is taken up interacting with other people. (age 49)

It took me a while to pluck up the courage to ring. I didn't want anyone to think I was wanting to talk about my relationship with my mother, that I was a mummy's boy or had any problems in that direction. (age 44)

Some progress has been made in diminishing the fear of this shameful tag. It is now possible for a young man to be unconscious of the risk it might pose. The prospect of being called a 'mummy's boy' had not even crossed Trevor's mind:

I got in touch because the night before your notice, I'd been discussing parental influences with my flatmate . . . I have a very strong and sound relationship with my mother. I understand the concern about being a 'mummy's boy', but I've never . . . it didn't even enter my head. But, yes, it is something that fellows do worry about. Most men react, not negatively, but nonchalantly, *to their mothers. Yes, many do worry about being seen as a 'mother's boy' even in their own minds. (age 28)*

Initially, Trevor had been confident that he could round up others who would be happy to take part and he took away a bundle of questionnaires. Three weeks later, he had only failure to report.

I gave them to some fellows at work who I thought might be willing. When I checked back, I picked up a reluctance to talk. I acted casual, laid-back, and we had a laugh, but I thought afterwards, 'None of these fellows is going to ring up'. But it's not for lack of feelings. I'd chosen them because I thought they would co-operate. They've given hints about how important their mother is—one fellow in particular . . . his father died when he was young so his relationship with his mother is almost a substitute for his father. She was in hospital recently and he was making all the arrangements. But I picked up a real reluctance from him and I thought, 'Well!'. I just think it's a reluctance to talk to others about what is a . . . very intimate thing probably. It's somewhat akin to asking men about their relationship with their wives. I think men of our age [late twenties] might be the most reluctant. I could see younger fellows, perhaps, being more willing, and older men, but at this age . . . I don't know why. These were the ones I thought would be the most promising. Now I'm uncertain about asking others. And I've been looking at my own motives. I don't know why I'm doing it. I'm not particularly outgoing by nature but this is something I felt was important. Something worthwhile. I've got very interested in it now. And the reaction of my sisters encouraged me as well. All of them have said, 'What a great idea. Well done.'

Opinions varied about what constituted a 'mummy's boy' and who was to blame. A 37-year-old plasterer was even-handed in his judgment.

To me a mummy's boy is one who not only can't and won't do without mum but, just as importantly, won't be let go by a clutching mother. Both are to blame. I can't say I've seen examples first-hand, but I have heard of the odd case or two. I don't class myself as a mummy's boy because, although I would, of course, be sad at the passing of my mother, I am ready to live on happily.

A man in his fifties who had firmly thrown off his strong-minded mother's control and was comfortable enough to have her living with his family, saw men's fears originating in homophobia: 'Some of the poofter-bashers don't know what they are do they?' But he tended to blame mothers for a relationship which attracted the accusation.

> *I've got friends, men in their forties, who are still mother-dominated and I see them as 'mummy's boys'. I think that's a legitimate criticism, [but] I think the term 'mummy's boy' is sometimes used incorrectly. It can be because the sons are still children, or they're substitute companions. I don't see it as the result of a bad relationship with a father, or as the son's fault. I think it's manipulative mothers.*

Fists settled Sean's childhood battles. From a tough working-class background, his firm views about what was appropriate between mothers and sons were completely aligned with mainstream masculine conditioning, revealing the traditional intolerance for anyone who failed to fit the pattern. In Sean's eyes, there was no excuse for a man who had not broken with his mother. With such strong feelings, he had to conquer his own reluctance about being seen as a 'mummy's boy' in order to volunteer for this study.

> *If I say someone is a 'mummy's boy', it's a derogatory term. I'm usually describing someone—either a child who runs to his mother for every slightest thing, or an older person, say over twenty-five, who is accompanied everywhere by his mother, or lives with his mother unmarried at the age of thirty plus, who goes on holiday with his mother . . . I tend to think there's something wrong with them, that they're weaklings and not independent. They can't break the strings from their mothers. To me, they're not men in my definition of a man. It is more the son's fault. I think it comes from a bad relationship between father and son and the mother being over-protective. In many cases, you can see a lot of emotional blackmail, especially in the older men who are totally blackmailed by their mothers. I know a pilot who's trying to have his airline's rules changed so he can take his mother on holiday. I think he's doing it because his mother's pressuring him. Another friend of mine, a solicitor, stayed at home with his mother and father, but he can't*

> *maintain a relationship with a woman. He certainly isn't gay, but his mother comes before everybody . . . and he came before his father in his mother's eyes. When his father died, they sold the big house and bought another. I said to him: 'Now's your chance to leave, get a flat'. But he resented me saying it. He was going with mummy and that was that . . . This terrible imitation of mother love is really just selfishness—and immaturity. I can't stand the sight of it. (age 44)*

The masculine viewpoint is not completely astray. Sean accurately identifies elements which cause much difficulty in the mother–son relationship. But his scorn and intolerance, his assumption that any but the most marginal role for a mother is a matter of shame, arise directly from masculine conditioning.

What men—and mothers—ultimately fear is homosexuality. But only some 'mummy's boys' are homosexuals. The epithet is equally applied to heterosexual boys who lack muscle, who are physically weak; boys who prefer chess to football; boys who refuse a fight; boys who, for whatever reason, cannot live up to the uncompromising yardstick of masculinity. David was like that. He was also homosexual.

> *The 'mummy's boy' syndrome? Oh yes, we've all suffered from that at some time or another. To me, it meant being different, not wanting to (or being able to in my case—I wear glasses) join in the rough and tumble of football and the like, being 'sensitive', not being part of the male group. Children are cruel towards those who are different for whatever reason. I've been labelled 'mummy's boy' in my time and so have others that I know. It hurts for a while, but it does prepare you for what comes later. Also, it is just as true that some of the most gay men I know would never have been called a 'mummy's boy'. (age 28)*

Little has changed and much of the change that has occurred is superficial or uncertain. Fear of being seen as a 'mummy's boy' still makes male children wary of their mothers' affection. And masculinity still so conditions mothers' expectations that even a woman who was consciously raising her sons against convention was confounded by her success. 'Henry is twelve. He will give me a hug and kiss in front of his friends. Sometimes I feel embarrassed, but he doesn't.' (age 41) Forty years earlier, compliance with masculine conditioning would have almost certainly made this mother tell her son not to kiss her, to say, as another woman did in the early 1980s, that he was 'too big for that now'. This example was proffered by a woman who was consciously seeking to change. It is also a sign of the general progress which has been made on this issue. If the boy takes the initiative, few mothers today will rebuff him whatever their private confusion.

Masculinity is not the only culprit. There have always been exceptions to the rule, springing from factors such as personality, family dynamics, favouritism: some mothers and sons are physically demonstrative towards one another all their lives despite any cultural restriction. The contributions to this study indicated that the chances of this have greatly increased with women's growing confidence and a softening in attitude to what constitutes masculine behaviour. There were a number of descriptions of exceptions to the rule, for example:

> *Being such a beautiful boy and being so loved by everyone, it was hard to chastise him. He would laugh at us and have us in fits too. He was very affectionate, always willing to have a cuddle. Even as a teenager, he would stand beside my chair and put his arms around me. When we visit him and his family today, we always have a great cuddle and hugs. He is not afraid of showing his affection to us. (mother 67, son early thirties)*

More common then, and now, is a boyish instruction to his mother to keep her distance, most particularly in public. An appreciation of masculine conditioning makes the strictures of young males understandable, but is it fair? And should women continue to acquiesce when it hurts so much and contains such derogatory implications? Popular wisdom justifies boys' distancing as a reaction to 'silly', over-protective, fussy, unduly emotional maternal behaviour. But this is a masculine viewpoint and it does not sustain close examination. All types of mothers are treated this way, including perfectly sensible, self-controlled, dignified women. Mothers' behaviour is not the trigger to boys' retreat. That is, and always has been, an initiative of masculinity.

10 Post-1960s mothers

The majority of mothers who took part in this project were born during the war or shortly afterwards. By the 1990s, their child-rearing period was either coming to an end or had recently finished. They were aged predominantly between the late thirties and early fifties. Their sons ranged from teens through to the mid-twenties.

A particularly striking difference between this generation of women and their own mothers was the way in which new technology had changed the balance between housework and childcare. Active maternal participation, rather than support as an onlooker, was one of the major variations between the post-war years and the post-1960s decades. The younger mothers were not simply observers or background organisers. No longer swamped by household chores and less constrained by concern about 'appropriate' female behaviour, they felt free to join in. Their sons, as well as their daughters, experienced childhood with a female parent who actually took part in their activities and shared their enjoyment.

Education created another major difference between the two eras. Overall, the younger maternal generation were better educated and more sophisticated than their predecessors although only a minority had attended university before they became mothers. Many of the middle-class took up extra study after marriage but all of them became more worldly through the influence of television and, increasingly, travel. The gap in experience between a mother and her son narrowed.

Feminist influence was responsible for enlarging women's educational goals. It also triggered a debate which was to rage both at a personal level and in the community. The status of full-time motherhood, which was previously unassailable in women's own minds, suddenly seemed doubtful. Was it enough? Should they combine being mothers with outside work? Through the decades of their mothering, an intense female argument oscillated this way and that, the women's indecision aided, abetted, or hindered from the sidelines by men. Some of the fiercest battles were hidden from sight, fought within women themselves as they tried to reconcile their girlhood conditioning with their adult hopes.

Researchers Jan Harper and Lyn Richards tracked the

establishment in women's minds of two equally negative—and self-imposed—stereotypes about their role. A group who were themselves wives and mothers described the 'typical' full-time housewife as 'dowdy, dull, lazy, boring' while the stereotype working mother was labelled 'abrasive, ambitious, selfish, arrogant or simply hassled'.[47] Containing overwhelmingly more negative qualities than positive, these derogatory images were conceptualised by women about each other as a result of the broadening of their choices. They reflected the internal debate they were holding with themselves which reached its height during the 1970s.

Exemption from these two unpleasant stereotypes could be achieved, but the way out was the same for both: emphasise motherhood. Sociologist Lois Bryson summarised the research done by Harper and Richards in the late 1970s.

> For women who stayed at home, exemption was claimed by emphasising mothering and the temporary nature of their full-time home role. The most common qualification exempting working mothers from the typical image was working part-time, or only after children reach school age, and of course making sure one's work does not deprive the children . . . In both cases, women were expected to subject their own interests to those of their children.[48]

Almost without exception, the mothers who took part in this study fell into one of the categories described above. Few were self-designated feminists. Dedicated career women, or full-time working women of any occupation were equally sparse. The majority worked outside the home for at least some period but, in the main, they did so part-time and with the rationalisations detailed by Bryson. Those who were full-time mothers usually explained their choice in the terms Bryson mentioned. Women's jobs brought them enjoyment and pride, but they were also a source of guilt. As a result, many fell into the trap of straining to perform their multiple roles perfectly, just as they had sought to emulate the 'ideal' mother when that was their only role.

Full-time mothers were not guilt-free either. Confronted at every turn by women's new activities, some felt inadequate and resented the perceived pressure to join in. Many became defensive and, sometimes, stridently critical. In Australia particularly, the division of female opinion frequently detracted from the joy of achievement. It was a problem which American-born psychologist, Toby Green detected with an outsider's devastating accuracy: 'Australian women experience each other's gains as being a loss'.[49] In this context, the fellowship of women, which was initially such an attractive element of feminism, often struggles to survive and the lack of female encouragement increases the guilt of those who work.

Personal ambivalence prevented many women from accepting feminism but mothers of sons had some particular disincentives. Added to the general feminist denigration of motherhood was the double ambivalence caused by mothering 'the enemy' and, because feminism and femininity were assumed to be incompatible, feeling obliged to disavow one of the celebrated pleasures of having a son viz. the interaction of femininity with his masculinity.

Only the most committed women could be expected to transcend so many negatives. It was far too hard, far too complex, for most mothers—much easier to believe that feminism need not apply to sons. This solution also avoided the worry that feminist commitment might somehow compromise a boy's masculinity although very few women expressed this as a real concern. The majority never reached that point. Many pursued unattributed feminist lifestyles, some even called themselves 'feminists', but whatever their degree of personal commitment, most had mentally quarantined their boys from its effect. In many families, feminism was for mothers and daughters only.

Women's common response to whether feminism had affected the way in which they reared their boys was the assertion that because they *felt* equal as people, or expressed opinions about equal rights, their sons would absorb these attitudes also. For many, feminist influence began and ended with the belief that their own strong feelings were sufficient to shape their sons' views. Virtually none of them had analysed the question with any greater complexity although many worried that their partner's behaviour and their relationship with him contradicted what they said. And beyond the personal, most underestimated the degree to which the wider cultural forces were aligned against their own stance for equality. Married women blamed their partners for any sexist attitudes in their sons. Without a man in the house, single mothers were more conscious of the influence of external factors but most were utterly confused by the appearance of masculine or sexist traits in their son and marvelled that he should be 'like his father' even when man and boy hardly knew each other. Unable to explain this development satisfactorily, single mothers struggled with the problem of promoting a positive male identity while simultaneously combatting sexism. In this they were on the front line of the central dilemma for feminist sympathisers rearing young males who must survive and flourish in the world of men: how to find a balance between masculinity, particularly the best of masculine qualities, and the feminisation of social values. It is a conundrum for mothers of sons which has so far been virtually ignored. A 34-year-old single mother rearing two boys aged fourteen and eleven had been forced to confront its contradictions.

I do sympathise with some views held by the feminist movement and in the early days, I planned to bring my sons up not to be blatant chauvinists like other men in the family. However, they don't live in a vacuum and I find that outside influences affect their attitudes just as much as I do. As a single parent, it is a struggle to bring up two boys and keep the balance between teaching them to be men and yet reinforce non-sexist ideas.

Few women were sufficiently committed to feminism to make specific attempts to implement the movement's philosophy in rearing their sons. Those who tried found it a sobering experience. Ideology could too easily be received as nothing more than an irritant, sometimes even disparaged as maternal 'nagging' and the whole subject could become part of an ongoing adolescent tussle between mother and son. Invariably, there was also an obvious gap between theory and practice.

I am a feminist and I have taken a course in gender studies. I have tried to introduce feminist ideas at home. For a while John adopted these, but only to annoy the staff at his fairly traditional school! I have noticed that I am usually discussing ideals while preparing food for men. John finds having a feminist mum mostly

> *an embarrassment, but I am certain that some of my principles are percolating through. I constantly censor sexist language for instance. (age 42, two teenage sons)*

Household chores were one of the few feminist issues which did not make women feel ambivalent. Most mothers asserted firmly that these should be split equally between boys and girls with no sexist division of labour and, indeed, that a deliberate attempt should be made to cross traditional gender lines. Boys should learn to iron; girls, to replace a fuse. But, more noticeable than any attempt to redress the balance of jobs, was the basic aim that their daughters should not function in a serving role. In fact, work was not reallocated between the children. More often women changed their daughters' role without altering things for their sons. Beset by personal guilt at not being full-time housewives, overworked and short of time, they compensated—and found it simpler—to do everything themselves. Only occasionally did they admit the gulf between rhetoric and reality, but the latter was certainly substantiated beyond the evidence submitted here. In 1991, Michael Bittman's large scale study *Juggling Time* revealed how even full-time working women still bore the major portion of domestic responsibility. The family members who did least were teenage sons.[40]

Many women initially tried the feminist recommendations concerning reverse games and toys. They quickly gave up. The boys pushed dolls aside in favour of construction sets or cars and insisted on turning the nearest stick into a weapon. Mothers of all generations agreed that this type of feminist strategy was useless because 'boys would be boys' regardless of their best efforts to suggest otherwise. A mother in her mid-thirties with a son who was only five years old expressed the same sentiments as many others whose boys were already in their twenties.

> *I bought him a doll and he had no interest in it whatsoever. Yet at playgroup there's a black doll which he adores. I felt he should have the opportunity to nurture something. He has two furry toy rabbits and he talks about them like dolls. And 'Teddy' is popular. I've bought him a lot of cars because he's absolutely obsessed with them. It's coming from him. He 'drives' them around. He has a hill where they park. I always thought this was an environmental thing,*

> *but the more I talk to mothers of boys and girls, the more they say they thought it was due to environment until they had children. . . . But maybe, the children are more perceptive at an early age than you give them credit for.*

Twenty-five years of feminist examination has not produced any firm conclusions about the 'nature versus nurture' argument. It rages unabated among parents and professionals alike. Many women came to motherhood predisposed to believing that gender differences were due to nurturing but mothering a boy convinced them otherwise. Even if they were aware that some modern research indicated nurture was highly determinant, they gave it little credence against their personal interpretation.

Initially, it appears that boys have less to gain and more to lose from anything which might compromise their acceptance in the powerful male world. Research by June Statham found that that factor alone was a major deterrent to mothers 'tinkering' with the way boys are raised.[51] Most significantly, Statham's investigation concluded that:

> It is the emotional quality of the parent–child relationship which is one of the critical factors in non-sexist childraising.[52]

A relationship which begins with the dynamics of master and slave, however charming, will not lead to adult equality between the sexes.

Research carried out by Burns and Scott in 1989 revealed how strongly some young women feel about the need for equality in their relationships with the opposite sex. The research group of educated, middle-class women regarded the idea of marriage to a traditionally-minded man as 'intolerable'. Even two women of Greek background, one of whom specified that she was 'not a feminist' nevertheless told researchers that 'they could not abide a "bossy" man, nor one who wanted to be "king of the castle"'. These female 'trailblazers', as Burns and Scott designated them, were looking for partners who were 'egalitarian, supportive, non-dependent and able to look after themselves both practically and emotionally'.[53]

There was little evidence that mothers had addressed the implications of the feminist revolution. No one had considered what happens when girls are reared with aspirations which no longer complement those of boys, or if they did give it thought, no one knew what to do. The process which made boys sexist remained a mystery. Even the most intelligent of mothers missed the crucial role of the dynamics which they themselves had created. It was a severe shock when a woman from this generation discovered that, despite her deep personal convictions, her twenty-year-old son was perpetuating aspects of masculinity which she utterly disliked.

> *I am baffled by the success or failure of my role as a mother to my son . . . my greatest disappointment is that he upholds quite chauvinistic views towards women . . . when one has prided oneself on upholding liberated womanly views, the realisation that you have produced 'another one' is devastating . . . Where is it that we mothers go wrong? Could it be that we give conflicting signals to our children, particularly the male variety?'.* (age 46)

Teenage girls were illuminating about the dynamics operating between modern women and their sons. They described mothers who, like the earlier generation, are still in charge of daily discipline, responsible for setting the boundaries of behaviour, for making decisions on a myriad of topics from haircuts to clothes, to visits to the beach or the movies. They are the parent who usually decides rewards or punishments. In every respect, they are the disciplinarians on the spot—but, according to their daughters, they are not 'the boss'—at least, not in relation to their sons. Research by sociologist Paul Amato supports the anecdotal material contributed to this study.[54] Where boys are concerned it still takes 'a stern male voice' to pull them into line just as it did forty years ago.

Overwhelmingly, the girls said that fathers were the authority figures in boys' lives. Aged between thirteen and fifteen years, most of these female commentators were sisters, but their numbers included a few cousins or girlfriends whose opinions obviously reflected what they had been told by the boys. But even sisters, who loyally began by claiming that both parents disciplined their brothers, invariably added that their father acted as 'the enforcer'.

> *My father usually disciplines him, but my mother sometimes tries*

too. My father's got more 'power' over him. My brother reacts annoyed or angry to discipline. (girl age 13, brother age 14)

When he needs disciplining my Mum shouts at him, but if he doesn't listen, my Dad helps. (girl age 13, brother age 15)

My dad disciplines my brother the most by yelling at him, talking harshly to him and sometimes hitting him. My brother doesn't listen to my mother at all. He just laughs in her face. (girl age 15, brother age 12)

My father usually achieves the best results when disciplining, but Mum also does well. (girl age 13, brother age 10)

My Dad disciplines my brother sometimes, but Mum will sometimes stick up for my brother if she doesn't agree with Dad. My Mum also disciplines my brother, but she isn't as harsh with him. (girl age 14, brother age 12)

Parents may assume attitudes of equality and theoretically fathers may no longer be the undisputed head of the house, but mothers have the same trouble that they have always had in getting their sons to take them seriously. Watching her tiny mother's ineffectual attempts to control her brother aged eighteen, one girl decided that size was definitely a factor in the unequal battle.

My Dad disciplines him because my mother is too little, in a way, for her words to sink in. This isn't often though. But Mum does it when it is less important.

Given masculinity's respect for strength, it seems logical that it would affect sons' reactions to their mothers' attempts to exert authority. One of the sons confirmed this, recalling the advantage—and the impact—of his father's size.

Dad always made some time to be with his family so I am equally close to both. Occasionally, Mum would have to be peacemaker, but only over trivial disagreements. I think Mum made most of the rules, but it usually fell to Dad to apply them. His voice was louder and his physical presence larger and it seemed easier for him to get the desired result. Because of this, I believe he was stricter—at least, it felt like it. (age 30)

Teenage sisters pick it immediately when their mothers succumb to their brothers' charm.

> *They argue, but only if he doesn't get his own way. He swears a lot around Mum, never around Dad. Mum threatens him but she can never stay mad at him as he sucks back up to her. My brother doesn't get much discipline from Mum except threats, and he doesn't get that mad. But if Dad gets angry with him then he rebels (e.g. Dad says he's not allowed to do something, then he will go and do it). It's pretty ugly if Dad gets mad at him. (girl age 14, brother age 12)*

Fathers form their own opinions about the relationship between their partner and son. One man watched the old discrepancy being perpetuated between his toddlers, a boy aged four and a daughter who was six.

> *I do feel my wife is too soft with our son and very hard on our daughter. This could be because our daughter is like her and she understands her too well and damps down on her. Whereas our son is more like me. Perhaps she protects him because of it. I think she underestimates him and believes that boys have a less complex outlook on life. She is definitely over-protective physically. I tend to let him make mistakes and fall over so he'll learn, but my wife tries to stop this. (age 30)*

Contemporary mothers were not oblivious to their difficulties, but they were defensive about any suggestion that they treated their sons more leniently than their daughters. Their reactions ranged from anger and an immediate denial, to a considered personal appraisal, to dismay, amusement and guilt. Some suggested that because a child was the youngest it might have appeared to others that he was being favoured. A very few confessed that the old adage had, in fact, been true for them. One woman aged forty-four suggested its impetus was masochistic: 'I think it's easier to be indulgent on other-sex children, because being strict with a same-sex child is like being strict with yourself'. For another it arose entirely from gender assumptions: she felt obliged to 'perform' her maternal role to a higher standard for the benefit of a girl because she assumed that her daughter would regard her as a role model. Conversely, she could relax the rules with her son because there would be nothing in her feminine nature which a boy would want to emulate.

Stereotyped gender behaviour influenced and was reinforced by many modern mothers who continued the maternal tradition of acting 'softer' towards their sons to compensate for their partners' harshness. 'Overbearing', 'aggressive', 'unreasonable', 'dogmatic', 'inconsistent' were among the terms women used to describe their husbands' discipline. Most felt the men's approach was unsuitable, even the wrong way to exert control. Many were very unhappy about it. When fathers also made a great distinction between treatment of their daughters compared to their sons, the boys' mothers could be even more tempted to bias their own behaviour in the opposite direction.

> *If he was tough on Alex, but silly with our daughter, which he was, then I found myself being tougher on her than our son . . . that was because my husband was quite tough on him. He didn't need two of us to be like that. (age 50)*

A mother's ability to enforce discipline could be undermined by gender stereotypes or personal anxieties about conflict. Lack of change in masculinity made it harder still. Even confident mothers whose self-esteem was high, still had to struggle with boys whose conditioning was insisting that they must not let anyone 'beat' them, particularly not a woman. Simultaneously, the male culture continued to present women as less 'serious', less 'important', less 'formidable', less 'authoritative' and women themselves often reinforced this image by behaving as the culture asserted. Boys heard these messages in the 1950s. They hear them, only marginally altered, today.

Nevertheless, mothers were determined that their sons must accept women as equals. Those who worked took it for granted that their jobs would automatically contribute to this goal by demonstrating their individuality as people. They underestimated how their own pervasive maternal guilt detracted from their multiple roles. Women's attitude to their work and the way it was presented to their sons plainly revealed how boys were quarantined from the effect of feminism. A job which would be shared with a daughter as a skill, an achievement, a challenge or a source of pleasure and excitement, was more often than not presented to a son as a financial necessity and one which would be a source of extra benefits to *him.* Seeking his approval, mothers appealed to their boy's self-interest. They were also apologetic. When they took a job outside the home, it would be accompanied by anxious assurances that it would make no difference to his life.

One mother's story made it very clear that even small sons detected their mothers' ambivalence about working. After expressing her own belief that mothers should 'always be there', she added that her two young teenage daughters liked the fact that she worked, but then went on to describe, with what sounded suspiciously like pride, a primary school son who insisted: 'A mum should always be at home'. This inconsistency within one family was not unique. Daughters diluted what their mother said with their own interpretation of her actions, but sons, of whatever age, listened to their mothers' explanations and heard the guilt. It reinforced the cultural stereotype which was developing in their minds about what a 'real' mother should be like. Some felt entitled to disapprove of their own for breaking the rules. A signficant number of mothers reported that their boys initially resented their work, even when it was part-time and did not interfere with being home after school. Most added that the boys eventually 'got over it'.

Serious financial need cancelled a mother's guilt about working and eliminated apologies. Women who had no choice took less account of their son's opinion. He was made aware of the importance of his mother's job, but persuading him to approve was irrelevant.

> *I don't know how my eldest son feels about my work. When I had him I was part way through my apprenticeship and it never entered my head to give up. Then circumstances forced me to continue working. So, he has never known what it's like for me not to work. I can only assume that he would have wanted me to be there for him like some of his friends. Working for someone else made it impossible to attend daytime school functions. I would love to have been more involved because those times can never be repeated. (age 40, son 23)*

Effectively granted the right to approve, sons felt free to be quite proprietorial about their mothers' work. Women relayed their boys' opinions not only about whether they should work, but about what work they should do. Boys did not like their mothers doing a job they regarded as menial or inappropriate. They were ambivalent about mothers who worked with the handicapped, for instance, but, almost without exception, found the idea of the women as students very appealing. Many mothers described how their boys encouraged them to study. In fact the sons' enthusiasm suggested a link to their fathers, so many of whom longed for their mother to develop greater mental breadth and flexibility. A modern son tended to be blunt. 'Why don't you go out and do something, Mum, so you don't grow into a vegetable'. And, occasionally, enthusiasm tipped into pressure. Knowing her son would express his opinion for this project, one mother who had resisted heavy persuasion to study, said somewhat defensively: 'He may think it would have been good for my self-esteem, but the reality is that life would not have been so comfortable for the family if I had gone to university'. However dubious the attitudes there was, nevertheless, much evidence that the basic motive was the boys' eagerness to feel proud of their mothers. Scattered somewhat sparsely, but persistently, through the women's reports, were examples of young sons comparing, discussing, even bragging about their mother's work, with the same possessive pride that legend always maintained they took in their father's occupation.

A woman's guilt about working made her vulnerable to exploitation. Sons for whom their mother's job was another weapon in the battle for dominance exposed her weakness very easily. Wielding the concept of a 'proper' mother was guaranteed to make her abject and some boys could be detected using this idea as a means of control. The more guilty justification apparent in a mother's description of her work, the more likely it was that she would go on to describe a son who was either asserting general masculine disapproval about her job, or specifically using it as part of an ongoing feud. Not all objections were as ugly or as serious as this. Some were nothing but stubborn resistance from rebellious teenagers who wanted to deny their mother the pleasure of talking about her job. Occasionally, they would refuse even to acknowledge its existence. All these reactions played on a mother's lack of self-esteem and the boys' pressure for her to be a 'proper' mother was pervasively evident. Sometimes, a father's influence was also obvious.

> *I'm sure he sees me as a mother; figure of authority and provider of meals and other home comforts. He has managed to overlook my paid job. He never asks questions and looks disinterested when I chat about it. (age 40, son 19)*

> *I had secured a position working with adults who have physical or intellectual disabilities. I love my work. Chris hated it at first and would not recognise me when he saw me in the street. I must admit I can understand. And also he said, 'To think his mother had to work for money was terrible'. He was quick to remind me that 'Dad said I had lots of money and what did I want to work for? I should be home with the children during the school holidays'. I agree, but I didn't have this choice if I wanted to work. (age 45, son 20)*

Women are finally resolving their ambivalence about work and motherhood. Social researcher Hugh Mackay detected the trend in 1986 and Helen Glezer from the Institute of Family Studies confirmed it further in 1993.[55] The same pattern was apparent among the material submitted here. Mothers who work, whether by choice or circumstance, are doing so with more confidence. Newer mothers, although not always younger in years, are integrating their work into their family life. Without apology or defensiveness, they described the various ways it affected their sons and their own efforts to help the boys understand. Most of this group were conscious of the need for their children actually to experience the consequences of their work if it was to shape their attitudes. They were also aware of its value in helping the children form a three dimensional view of them. Working mothers are nothing very extraordinary to sons under about twelve years of age and their mothers, too, take it pretty much for granted. For some of these boys, fathers are filling the space left vacant in a domain once designated 'women only'.

> *It's one of the 'givens' of his life that his mother works and if he*

has opinions at all now, I suppose he wants me to have a secure job so I can buy him things. He did make one comment which I thought at the time must have come from my ex-husband. I was working part-time in order to pursue other interests too and he said: 'Why don't you just settle down and get a job like everybody else'. I thought it was an odd thing for him to say. Probably his father muttered it at some stage. I'm divorced, but we've never been in trouble, so the financial side of my work has never impinged on his life. I don't think there's anything about what I do which, in an eight-year-old universe, is terribly heroic. He's heard me on radio and he thinks that is fun. And he likes the fact I'm a librarian. He characterises me as a librarian and says: 'Oh, what else would I get for Christmas but a bag of books!'. Or, 'You should know about that. You're a librarian!'. But I don't think he even thinks about my occupation much. And he doesn't mention what his friends' mothers do, unless I ask about it. (mother 35, son 8)

During the boys' primary school years, contemporary mothers joined in many physical activities such as hikes, sailing, fishing, cycling and swimming, but these varied forms of exercise rarely included formal sport. Despite the liberation of the female role, women were fundamentally no more interested in sport than they had ever been. The significant difference among this generation of mothers was that, once the boys reached adolescence, many no longer felt obliged to pretend. In every way, sport emphasised male–female differences as surely as it did in earlier decades. The distinction once arose entirely at men's initiative, but in the 1970s and 1980s, women helped to perpetuate it. Few mothers of sons tried to find a way of enjoying sport. Only those who were sole parents really stretched themselves to bridge the gender gap. Married women were more than happy to delegate the whole subject to the boy's father.

I was never a football mother. I couldn't stand to go, or even play a good mother by pretending to enjoy it. I was so thankful to have a father around for that. I just couldn't relate to it. (age 50)

Fear that their child might get hurt was often apparent in what mothers had to say about sport, but it was not the common reaction. Disinterest was the most frequent explanation, with distaste for aggression also a factor. These specifically feminine reactions were reinforced by traditional masculine reluctance for mothers to be visible at all, which deterred some who might otherwise have watched their sons play, but many women refused to watch their sons' matches because they either were bored or disapproved. Some were derogatory as well. Their attitude allowed stereotyped images of active men and passive women, of 'macho' competition and timid females to flourish unchecked. Equally retrograde was a variation to the stereotype where female enthusiasm was expressed as feminine admiration for 'heroes'. However valid their reasons, by abdicating a balanced, positive attitude to their sons' sporting interests, mothers reinforced the traditional gender assumptions, talking equality on the one hand, but contradicting it in other ways. Many sons of the younger generation received mixed messages about sport despite its importance to them.

A most significant feature of the relationship between these women and their sons was the amount of conversation which occurred as though an entire generation never stopped talking. There were exceptions, of course. Hormones and conditioning made male children retreat as they had always done. And some mothers pressed too hard. Class differences were apparent also, the middle class leading the way in setting new patterns for communication between boy and woman while working-class families retained more of the traditional gender gap.

Mothers took their conversational role very seriously, their emphasis on doing the 'emotional housework' as gender-driven as their reaction to sport. They were enormously concerned to help their boy express his emotions. His own feelings and his ability to appreciate those of others were recurring topics. The following was typical in every respect, except in mentioning the boys' marriage, which most did not.

> *I encourage them to talk about their feelings, to really let people know what they are thinking as it can only be beneficial for them when they are married themselves. Communication is so important. (age 37)*

Many of this generation went further and tried hard to develop empathy in their boys as well. 'To develop sensitivity and compassion, I tried to help him put himself in the shoes of others who have needs'. (age 50)

Discussing a boy's feelings was the most frequent subject for conversation, but it was striking how widely the topics ranged. Virtually nothing was taboo. Women plainly no longer saw themselves in the role of 'God's police', but values and beliefs still featured, including formal religion. They concentrated on teaching their sons not to hurt others, which extended from not fighting at school, allowing for another person's point of view, or more sophisticated arguments for non-violence. The old instruction 'Go and hit him back' was barely evident. Movies, music, travel, food, current affairs and politics were popular subjects of common interest. Family relationships were still important and were often a vehicle for discussing a boy's feelings. Gardening was barely mentioned but there were hints it may enter the discussion when the boys establish their own homes, just as it did for an earlier generation. Many women claimed that they were prepared to discuss anything at all, even with very young children.

Some of the frankest, most wide-ranging conversations were described by single mothers, a pattern which was even more apparent when a teenage unmarried mother had virtually grown up with her child. One mother who had given birth at eighteen declared that everything was open for discussion with her son, including girlfriends.

> *My twenty-three-year-old and I discuss everything that's relevant. Drugs, sex, rock 'n roll. Seriously, we do talk about everything. There are no barriers. I worry about AIDS and young people. I let him know that I hope he is careful and uses condoms. We discussed drugs when he started high school and we still do now and then, nothing in depth because neither of us have experience with drugs. I do my gentle soap box bit about them. We talk about his childhood, his friends from the past. His job. There is nothing that I deliberately avoid . . . Oh yes, and we talk about his girlfriends and associated problems. I like to think I give him a female viewpoint. (mother 40, son 23)*

There have always been some boys who discovered books or a love of music in their mother's company and this younger generation were no different from their fathers, but it happened more frequently for them. Although the foundations for such a bond were often laid in early childhood, it was most likely to flower as the boys moved into their final years of schooling, or went to university. Many women reported that it helped their relationship make the transition from mother and child to one of equal adults.

> *We talk of politics, world affairs,* their *jobs and prospects,* their *women, clothes, art, the cats, cars, sex . . . the list goes on. No taboos. Beliefs, attitudes, rights of others, the ups and downs of* their *own lives are all discussed. (emphasis added) (mother 54, two sons early twenties)*

There was no similar high point if no mutual interests existed, or if the boy had grown up with a heavy emphasis on traditional masculinity which rejected things female. Sometimes a traumatic adolescence was both cause and effect, its wounds still raw in the boy well into his twenties. One mother described her cautious efforts to heal the antagonism which had developed during her son's teenage years.

> *We talk about his job, his sporting activities, some current affairs. I ask him about his social life. The communication lines are slowly opening up again. As there has been so much conflict, he wouldn't talk, and doesn't, about his feelings. He keeps it all inside. (mother 47, son 23)*

Even when there had been no conflict, there were few signs from any of the mothers that they expected their interest in what their sons were doing, thinking and feeling to be reciprocated. Some could be observed using their sons as confidantes rather than their husbands: '. . . she finds it easier . . . with me than my father, who is sometimes less interested'. But very few women nominated *their* work or *their* feelings as something they discussed with their sons. It was the exception rather than the rule for the conversation to work two ways. Both parties undoubtedly took pleasure in it, but the *needs* of only one were of concern.

Most women wanted the relationship to evolve to one of 'friendly equals' which recognised their own individuality too. Only a minority liked the idea of 'mother' as their enduring image.

Essentially, they were seeking a quality few listed in their maternal job description, nor mentioned as something which they hoped to develop in their sons. 'Respect' was not prominent in their thinking as it had been for their predecessors but, respect was, in fact, what they sought. Their version of respect was not a litany of manners which amounted to polite deference, nor was it a code of chivalrous behaviour, which disguised male assumptions that women's minds and emotions were as weak as their bodies. A modern mother wanted respect in the form of value for her opinions, for her purposes and, within her own definition, for her achievements. Appreciation of her needs. Overall, respect for her individuality.

No mother conceptualised her goal in such terms, but many had aspirations which collectively meant the same. In asserting, as the majority did, that their sons saw them as individuals, this is what they claimed. Yet few had tried to develop the necessary perspective in their boys. A generation before, women relied on husbands to inculcate respect in sons, but even then, some saw that a respect which was externally enforced was a poor substitute for the kind they generated themselves. Forty years on, respect was still envisaged as a passive tribute. Most of the younger generation granted their son the right to confer respect rather than asserting their entitlement to it. Invariably, the initiative lay with the boy. Equally significant, no woman apparently felt it necesssary for her son to earn *her* respect.

Many women spoke about their young adult sons with admiration as well as love. They were proud, as mothers have always been, of jobs and exam results, of things done and possessions acquired, but it was notable that these kind of achievements were usually of less importance. Their sons' personal qualities were the deepest source of pleasure for these mothers. They liked them as male people.

> *. . . He is extremely friendly . . . He is so strong and he is himself. . . . so natural. He never has to prove himself. Keeps his head. Has incredible courage. He gives me great faith in the future. (mother 50, son 20)*

The widespread celebration of the boys' final formative years was not necessarily an instance of women finding 'substitute husbands' in their sons. Similar enthusiasm and strong, friendly links were apparent among mothers with several sons and, by their own account, happy marriages. It often flourished in the years immediately before the boys left home, but there were some examples of friendships which continued comfortably after the boys moved out. One mother described her particular pleasure in the deliberate act of visiting and being visited. Her picture was very distinctly one of two friends rather than parent and child.

> *I enjoy his company and we have a few drinks and get into some pretty deep stuff about art, philosophy, dreams, and solve the world's problems. It's great being on* his *turf and, at other times, having him come and visit. (mother 49, son 24)*

Overall, the women's descriptions conveyed a picture of lively debates in which, unlike their own mothers, most had the confidence to join as intensely as the children. Their active physical involvement in the boys' primary years transformed for many into an equally vigorous intellectual involvement as the children matured. This generation of mothers continues as it began, as participants rather than observers.

Nevertheless, the long arm of Phillip Wylie's overwhelming, devouring, intruding 'mom' reaches down the years to restrain the daughters who were indoctrinated during the post-war decades from 'forcing' their 'unwelcome' presence on their sons. Some mothers still lack confidence in the relationship with their sons to an extent which makes them uncertain of their welcome.

> *If I pop in to see him at his flat, I wouldn't want him to feel that I have 'cornered' him on his own to interrogate him so I don't take too much of his time. (mother 54, son 26)*

The fear of being an overbearing mother is noticeably still around, even if carefully rationalised.

11 Sons—the younger version

The male generation now aged between early teens and late twenties was born into a very different environment from their fathers. Their society was broader, more complex, less conformist. The celebration of individuality and difference which had begun in the 1960s among the intellectuals, spread rapidly throughout the socio-economic layers. Definitive standards were replaced by choice; rigid community morals by flexible personal ethics; security and familiarity by mobility and uncertainty. Technological change ensured that childhood was no longer centered on the neighbourhood, the suburb or the village and these sons grew up with wider physical and mental horizons than their parents.

Families were also different and they continued to change, becoming steadily less patriarchal, less hierarchical and formal—more casual. Male and female roles were under scrutiny and in dispute, with change accelerated by marital breakdown. Post-war children may have grown up with mothers who were widows, but increasing numbers of late-century children lived with mothers who were divorced.

The male experience of the mother–son relationship changed substantially. The consensus which emerged from these younger sons' opinions was a reversal of the past. The percentage which once ran 70:30 negatively about a man's mother, had turned right around to run approximately 70:30 positively. Most sons of this age group spoke enthusiastically about their mothers, the percentage as well as the tone of the assessment holding good among those who explored the subject in some depth and those who answered a briefer questionnaire. These sons loved their mothers, as their fathers had loved theirs, but the younger generation also liked them.

Asked what they liked best about these women, the sons began by nominating qualities which were traditionally female and maternal. 'Helpful', 'caring', 'supportive' recurred most frequently. 'Always there' was praised too, but much less often than their fathers had mentioned it about their own mothers and far less often than contemporary mothers (who rate it highly), would fondly imagine. While most appreciated their mother's interest in their lives, the women's firmly held view that their boys were bursting with conversation when they arrived home appeared no more true than a tired man or, more recently, a tired woman, returning from work and longing for some solitude to 'recover' from the outside world. Those boys who did regard 'always there' as a positive factor which deserved mention, were not necessarily the children of full-time mothers. A lawyer's son could also say confidently: 'She is always there when I need her. She cares and listens'. It appeared that, by adolescence at least and possibly earlier, sons defined 'being there' differently to mothers, their interpretation resting on emotional availability rather than physical presence. And their reaction cannot just be dismissed as sexist. A young man whose mother *and* father had been deeply involved in his life said: 'Both parents' love felt like a burden'.

The importance which mothers placed on being 'involved' in their children's lives also appeared to be something of a mixed blessing for the sons. If the involvement was too intense, the boys felt their personal space was being invaded. This criticism was not just a complaint from boys in mid-adolescence, although it was significant among that group. It surfaced among sons who were both older and younger than teenage. Some felt besieged by their mothers' interest.

> *. . . she is interested and she is interested. I know there are things she will be very interested to hear and it pleases me to tell her . . . Then, the worst is she is always interested, asking questions, probing, prying. It depends on how I am feeling . . . (age 22)*

Unlike their fathers, these sons did not dismiss their mothers' attempts to be involved as 'meddling'. Most of them did not lose sight of the women's loving intent and generally the relationship was resilient enough to withstand the aggravation. Nevertheless, they disliked the intrusion. 'Too many questions', 'interrogates my friends', 'thinks she can read my thoughts'.

Hugh Mackay found the same pattern when he researched teenagers and their parents in 1988. Commenting on the debates among some psychologists that the nuclear family imposes strain because the emotional spotlight falls more intensely on each member, Mackay confirmed:

> The evidence . . . certainly bears out this proposition. One of the great emotional needs of contemporary teenagers is for privacy: their own space, their own friends, their own values, their own money . . . symbols of privacy are crucial in the struggle to acquire an independent identity. Accordingly, invasions of that privacy (by parents or by siblings) generate enormous resentment and hostility.

Significantly, Mackay also found that while parents acknowledge their teenagers' need for privacy, '. . . they often appear rather insensitive to it, or even amused by it'. Three out of the four direct quotes which Mackay reproduced to illustrate this point described the reactions of sons.[56]

The mothers of this generation overwhelmingly nominated 'love' as the most important aspect of their maternal role. In doing so, they expressed both change and continuity because the older generation, too, rated love as essential, but not so far ahead of other qualities and not so urgently. The older group regarded discipline as almost equally important. By comparison, the mothers of the post-1960s decades barely mentioned discipline. To them, love mattered above everything else—the importance of giving it and displaying it.

The measure of the women's success was their children's response: almost without exception, this male generation felt loved, but the detail they proffered about their mothers' behaviour revealed more similarities with the past than might be expected. It by no means always involved explicit maternal statements, or physically demonstrative behaviour of the kind their fathers so longed for. According to these sons, their mothers' style varied. Many women did find a way to say 'I love you', some putting it in writing by sending cards or notes, others actually telling the boys. But the numbers who deliberately verbalised their affection were matched by many others who expressed it through their behaviour as generations of mothers had done before them. Despite this traditional reticence, their loving feelings were recognised and understood.

Critical scrutiny of the sons' answers suggested that they must take some credit for the transformation at the emotional core of the mother–son relationship. Their descriptions of how their mother showed her feelings, revealed that the young men themselves were more perceptive than their fathers. A middle-aged son might need a therapist's help to recognise the loving look in his parents' eyes, but almost without exception, the younger generation could detect it for themselves.

> *As a family, we are warm but not greatly affectionate . . . I know Mum loves me just because I know. Its expression is in attitude and* how *something is said rather than what is said. In doing, not telling. I suppose that we are not comfortable enough with ourselves to say 'I love you'. About as openly affectionate as we become is a kiss on the cheek for some special reason . . . (age 28)*

> *[It is] in her face, her smile, because she says so. And I always felt well accepted and pretty well understood for who I am . . . (age 25)*

> *She tells me. And I can see it in her look sometimes. It is not through cooking, or doing my washing when I'm home, or any practical thing, but by the way she treats me as an equal, the way we talk, the way she smiles. When she puts it into words I feel embarrassed by the inadequacy of the word 'love' and by being told. There is no need for her to say it, though, I suppose like her I often simply have to tell her. (age 22)*

> *I know she loves me because she is always thoughtful in what she does for me. (age 18)*

Mothers have not changed in some respects. The earlier generation cooked their boys' favourite food. This generation remembered to buy it when they went shopping. But the younger women were more fortunate than their predecessors because their sons did not miss their gestures of affection. Changes in women's roles generally had made what a mother did more visible. In that sense, the younger men were less inclined to take their mother's services for granted and could more easily recognise the feeling behind her thoughtfulness. The feminist debate had reached their ears, even though most of their mothers had disavowed it. 'She expresses her love in praise, by taking the extra time to get some sort of food I said I liked, or a book . . .' (age 19).

The ambivalence of some boys showed that stereotypical masculinity still hurts the relationship. As in the past, it erupts most viciously when it conflicts with a mother who has not loosened the protective reins: 'She treats me like a mummy's boy . . .' (age 14). But mothers too can be badly hurt. In the following case, the culprit at least remembers that it was he who stopped the affectionate behaviour. Perhaps this memory and his underlying confidence in his mother's love will insulate him against feeling deprived in later years.

> *Mum doesn't really show her feelings for me, but I know she cares. I don't want a Mum who hugs and kisses and I told her this years ago. I know she loves me because of all the support she's given me over the years. (age 19)*

Another example of the emotional distance which masculinity exaggerates was provided by a young man who was already well into his twenties. His mother was firmly categorised into the past and he summarised their relationship dispassionately: 'She does not show any strong feelings for me. I believe she cares about and for me, but we are *not very close*'. Only one son in this age group reiterated the plaintive cry of the earlier generation that he felt unloved. Significantly, his mother held strong traditional views about what was suitably masculine and how it should relate to femininity. Perhaps her determination to impose those stereotypes conflicted with her son's personal qualities, making his real self feel unvalidated. The result was a young man who said he experienced 'some sort of unlovingness'. Struggling to define what he meant more precisely, he added: 'I know she loves me. She just doesn't have a good way of showing it'. He was reminiscent of that earlier generation who were subjected to such intense masculine socialisation, men whose minds told them that they were loved, but whose hearts were not convinced.

All kinds of stereotypes put the relationship between mother and son at risk, including assumptions about 'typical' mothers and 'good' mothers. The comments which sons made revealed that contemporary women still misread the masculine perspective on their mothering. Sons' interpretation of maternal behaviour often does not match up with women's imagination. Boys are still caught between concepts which disparage the 'typical' mother and the ideal of a 'proper' mother. The typical can be everyone's stereotype of the loving, unselfish mother but, to males, she is more often a creature to be derided. The contributions revealed that the legendary unselfish qualities of the role still make boy children feel uncomfortable. They do not perceive it as noble self-sacrifice but, instead, experience the ambivalence of loving someone who appears, in their eyes, to have so little self-respect.

> *What I like best and least about my mother is a total contradiction, because what I love* and *hate are one and the same—her unselfishness.*

In general, modern sons struggle to hold their own mother dear in a society which has little regard for mothers. Too often, their conundrum is accentuated by their own mother's attitude to her peers.

The male culture may have originated the disparagement of mothers but, insidiously woven throughout the contributions to this book, was evidence of women's collusion in the denigration of their maternal role. Not intentionally, not consciously, but defensively. Aware in the recesses of their hearts and minds that the common image disadvantages mothers, a woman may counter her son's perception of the 'typical' mother by aligning herself with the male viewpoint and disparaging other mothers. In a myriad small ways she emphasises her difference from the 'typical'—in throw-away remarks, in direct criticism, by contrasting her own special virtues. In the process, sometimes just by implication, she helps to perpetuate a derogatory image of mothers in general. The traditional ideology of motherhood is thus sustained, but at the expense of women's human reality and at the cost of confusing sons. No generational change was apparent on this topic.

If boys cannot find evidence which counters what the male culture tells them to expect of women then, given the derogatory context in which their opinions are formed, the chance that they will respect their mothers is remote. Against such an ambiguous background, praise from teenage sons is all the more heartwarming. A nineteen-year-old, who gave his mother a particularly hard time, came out the other side of adolescence with very positive feelings towards her. Her occupation was not important, nor was her mothering style. To this boy, the most significant feature of the battle was the way his mother refused to be a walkover in the masculine struggle for supremacy.

> *What has Mum achieved that I admire? She brought me up! I respect the achievement of bringing children up. Mum always states that she hated being the father figure, but she is a natural fighter, whether she liked it or not. She is very tough. I respect her a lot.*

Given a choice of descriptions of how they felt about their mothers, contemporary teenage boys did not readily choose 'admiration' or 'respect'. One teenager's reply illustrated how misleading such terms could be anyway. Initially, he was unequivocal in claiming that he respected and admired his mother.

> *Raising kids is an achievement anyone would be proud of. I'm very proud of this achievement by my mother. She is only tough in situations such as parties, staying out late, the usual parenting rules—or they are in this house. I respect her for her decisions, even if I think they are wrong. (age 15)*

On further examination of his entire contribution however, this strong personal tribute is revealed as very much shaped by a general notion about motherhood. Replying to a question deliberately designed to probe background attitudes, he riposted firmly:

> *I agree with mother love being unique, but it does demand something. It demands I respect and listen to my mother and respect her points of view.*

More illumination about the limits—and the inequality—of that respect, was contained in his reply to the questions about discipline. After describing both his parents as strict, he added: '. . . when my father yells, I listen. Whereas I don't always when my mother yells'.

One curious mother bluntly put the question of respect to her two teenage sons. Their replies are a fair indication of the cultural as well as the personal disadvantages which mothers have to surmount in male eyes.

> *I asked them, 'Why do you respect Dad (all men) more than me (all women)?'. These are their answers: (I took the lack of objection to my question to mean they agreed with it!) Elder son, age 17: 'We know you better, know what you think about things . . . how old-fashioned you are. Dad doesn't tell us what he thinks, so we*

can't disagree'. Younger son, nearly 15: 'They (meaning all women I presume), restrict us'. Silence, then the second statement made probably for entertainment value. 'They think they save us from our fate'.

It was noticeably easier for a son to agree that he admired or respected his mother when he did not have to pass judgment on her parenting at the same time. Contrasting the older and younger generations revealed this very clearly. Sons from the 1950s had no choice but to evaluate their mothers in their maternal role: 'reared six children', 'I suppose she has fulfilled what I perceive to be a good mother', 'maintaining a family of seven after my father was killed', 'I don't know whether I respect her . . . if only her understanding had been greater', 'inner strength and also her high moral standards'. In themselves, these tributes often sounded admiring enough but, in the overall context of the older sons' responses, it was impossible not to conclude that a fair number had taken refuge in society's definition of motherhood which helped them to find something to admire. When an alternative was available, sons of all ages nominated their mothers' achievements outside the home. Younger men who had this option more often were more readily admiring. They could avoid the ambivalence caused by passing judgment on the women's parental success in their own lives and external yardsticks, such as occupation, income or title, were concrete evidence that society endorsed their personal opinion. This was the benefit which a woman's outside work could bring to the mother–son relationship—not as a role model, as it was for daughters (although these younger sons did not automatically exclude their mothers as role models), but by providing the boys with something about their mother which was understood and valued in their male world.

I admire just one thing—she has managed to set up her own business . . . I admire her for just having the plain inspiration to get up and do something like that. She did not really know too much about the business side, only the production, but now, having started this business she has learnt a lot more about business matters. I do respect my Mum, but I would never call her 'tough'! I would use a less strong word in the way she has managed to bring up a family. I do respect her though and, for the most part, I always listen to what she has to say. (age 20)

I admire the way she manages to save from her income and respect her hard work. I wouldn't call her tough. (age 18)

I definitely think my Mum's tough. She is very sensitive underneath and can get hurt, but when she knows she is right she will follow something through till the end. She had a tough time building up her career, but she has done extremely well mainly because of her determination. This taught me a valuable lesson as I was growing up. (age 21)

I strongly admire my mother's work and the fact she never chose to work in a bank or sales job for twenty years and slowly move up some promotional ladder. She always takes very taxing jobs that deal directly with down-to-earth emotional, family and human problems . . . She's done the lot—marriage guidance counselling, working with sexually-abused children, social work, adoption, rehabilitation officer, etc. She's done so much, I don't even know what she's doing now. I always get asked what she does because I often talk about her and I have to say, 'I don't know' or, 'She works with people, ya know' . . . I really respect her for the relationship she has with all her kids' friends, who vary dramatically . . . I could describe so many of my mates who all ask about her, visit her, and reckon she's a real good sort. They say: 'She's a real great lady, man. How did you turn out to be such an arsehole?'. (Of course they're joking, I think?) (age 21)

On the testimony of these sons, mothers did not need to worry that their job might be detrimental to the relationship. Generally, it was noticeably to a mother's advantage and made her son admire her. A twelve-year-old, for instance, was entering adolescence with a confident and concretely-based admiration for his mother, which should provide a useful counter to any subsequent personal tussles between them.

Yes, I admire my mother. She has made our vineyard work well by planning and by pulling everything together and always looking for a good balance between what we've got to do and what we want to do. I think that balance *is a good thing. Sometimes I don't pay her respect because I don't do something as soon as she tells me to.*

She is pretty tough sometimes, but most of the time she is very caring.

Whether working outside the home or choosing to be full-time mothers, women benefit from having sons with a discriminating perception about human nature. A significant number of the younger generation displayed this quality and they included several who were very conscious of the effects of gender conditioning. In analysing what being a man was really about, they were developing the ability to distinguish between facade and reality. It was still easier to admire their mother for some accomplishment outside the home, but they had the psychological capacity to understand her as a three dimensional person in her context and it was notable how this understanding bred tolerance and respect.

Has my mother achieved anything which makes me really admire her? Yes, well, she brought us up on her own. She's got the respect and love of the people around her and she's really taken on a new lease of life over the last couple of years, new activities, hobbies, speech-making, getting out and about. Oh yes, and I suppose her outlook on life. Do I respect her? Yes. Could I ever call her tough? Yeah [slightly surprised]. I think it takes real toughness, a huge amount, to be totally vulnerable. They're the people I really regard as truly tough—someone who is open. To be that open you need a central core of unshakeable belief in either love or other people, which those who are less tough don't have. They [just] have shells to try and put the tough on the outside. (age 25)

Among the older age group, it was rare to find a son who commented that his mother's judgment was good, but the comment, 'she is usually right' occurred with increasing frequency among the younger men. Many had real respect for their mother's judgment and trusted her as a sounding board. Commonsense, pragmatism, integrity and flexibility have always been qualities which sons valued in their mothers and the younger generation were no different in this respect to their fathers, but they found what they needed more frequently and their admiration was obvious. In a sparse but noticeable trend among the youngest of them, lay the ultimate tribute: thirty years ago, it would have been unthinkable for a teenage boy to either say, or even think to himself, 'I want to be like my mother', but sisters reported that a couple of these boys did. And a schoolteacher could see it happening.

> *It depends on their background, of course . . . but astute male children are making the best of both worlds . . . Boys identify with mothers who are independent, free-thinking, nice people, not only for security and emotional reasons, but also because they happen to like their mothers as people. These are mothers who . . . actually present themselves to their sons as people without any overt 'being Mother'. Their sons look at them and think, 'Well, that seems a nice person to be, so I'll take some of those qualities and Dad's given me my male identity, which I need because basically I'm male'. If he also likes his father as a person, then some of the really great things about males and females come together in the child. There are some cases where you think, 'What a great kid', because the parents have managed to get rid of this bullshit about gender identification and have come across to their children as people. Every now and again, they need to act like Mum and Dad, but generally, women who show their uniqueness as a person are the ones the kids are really attracted to. I don't see a pattern. I just think the women need to be fairly secure in themselves. If they've chosen to be a traditional full-time wife, they need to be comfortable with it. And if they've chosen to have a career too, they need to be comfortable with that.*

Analysing whether or not sons' feelings for their mothers include admiration or respect is important because, without those elements, there is no basis for equality between them. And it will be the dynamics of the relationship on which equality rests because the boys have no commitment to feminism. They have inherited all their mothers' ambivalence towards the subject, the very word conjuring up the same anti-men, anti-motherhood, anti-feminine images. Their support and their knowledge begins and ends with a vague wish for fairness and equal opportunity. Their wives will be left to discover whether or not the behavioural change which feminism triggered in the mothers who disavowed it had profound effects on their male children despite the older women's doubts.

The suspicion that mothers had not reared their sons to give emotionally as well as receive was confirmed by the boys' responses. Only a very few young men had realised that mutual nurturing was desirable between the sexes. The following comment from a son aged twenty-one was exceptional: 'She is a good listener and often solves problems for me. I like to think I do the same for her'. Generally, mothers had worked to develop more emotional capacity in their sons from a presumption that it required female expertise and, given the contemporary gender gap in emotional capability, most really had no choice. But this emphasis was, at least partially, contradictory to what they were hoping to achieve. Andy Metcalf, writing in *The Sexuality of Men* described the probable consequences. For men to identify their needs, he said:

> . . . involves learning to identify our individual problems and taking responsibility for them, rather than blaming others for them, unless they are actually to blame. We no longer see others as the source of *our* own feelings and emotions, expecting them to make us feel better. There is a traditional vision of relationships in which both partners are seen as incomplete in themselves: they come together to find a new completeness. This means seeking in others what we have never learned to give ourselves. This can have deep sources in childhood if as boys we are looked after by mothers who never give us the space to find ways of nourishing ourselves, but are always anxious to do things for us. Then we never learn to take a very basic responsibility for ourselves. This has to do with cooking and cleaning, but it also has to do with learning to identify and fulfil—as opposed to dominating and suppressing—our own emotional needs. This helps produce an expectation of women as people *who take the emotional initiative* in relationships. (emphasis added.)[57]

Few fathers of this era had the benefit of childhood exploration about personal feelings of the kind that their sons experience and, as fathers, most took little part in the dialogue between their wife and son. In fact many were virtually excluded from it and their absence left the space for it to flourish even more. Whether from work or divorce or feelings of inadequacy, this generation of fathers continued to leave the emotional housework almost entirely to their wives who, with regard to their sons, gave every sign of accepting it willingly. The net result may be that their sons, who have become so much more sensitive and expressive, nevertheless have still grown up with the expectation that women will 'take the emotional initiative in relationships'.

One of the most positive indications for the future is the great change in sons' feelings about spending time with their mothers. Parent–child friction, 'typical' adolescent resentments, still occurred and there were a few replies which, in their brevity as well as their overall context, suggested a young man taking refuge from an unpalatable truth, but the widespread discomfort and boredom of the previous generation had undoubtedly vanished. In general, sons today welcomed their mothers' company and enjoyed their conversation.

The characteristic which seemed to be rated most highly in their mothers was 'understanding'. Many just left it at that single word. Some elaborated to: 'understands my needs', '. . . my point of view', '. . . what it is like to be a teenager'. Given that so many of them were adolescents, it was a major tribute to a generation of mothers for successfully maintaining communication through a potentially difficult period. Terms like 'meddling' or 'interfering' were noticeably absent from this group. Either mothers' behaviour had changed or the yardstick by which sons judged them had altered. Perhaps both.

As might be expected, the teenagers' reactions were the most mixed, their desire for privacy sometimes conflicting with the pleasure of talking things over with their mothers. But even this group was overwhelmingly positive, 80 per cent saying that they enjoyed their mother's company. Many of the positive answers were completely unqualified, but about 25 per cent added the reservation, 'sometimes', 'most of the time', or 'usually'. The group included a number who lived only with their mothers because their parents were divorced, but their opinions were no different to the sons living in intact families, although several mentioned that they were having more conversations with their mother since the family break-up.

I enjoy my mum's company and we normally go for walks, go to the beach, or just watch TV or cook. My relationship with her has changed over the years because when she yells at me, I yell at her.

But I don't like this so I am changing so we can love each other again. (age 14, mother 'secretary')

I enjoy my mum's company. I can sit and talk with her. We talk about school, her job and what we could do if we won the lottery. Quite often we see movies together. And she comes to the school activities I do. (age 14, divorced mother in advertising)

I enjoy my mother's company and we usually talk about school or financial problems. My relationship with my mother has changed. This is alright because she wants my personality to grow unlike some mothers who dominate their children. (age 13, mother 'interior designer')

I enjoy her company. We usually go shopping and talk about what happened throughout the day. Our relationship has grown better over the years. It has changed by the way we understand each other better, which I think is great. (age 16, mother 'housewife')

Yes, I do enjoy my mother's company. The only thing that bugs me is I can't talk about the facts of life, or girls, as I go shy and she goes gooey. (age 14, mother 'housewife')

Teenage sons were not angels of co-operation: the emotional withdrawal, or the distinctive, touchy, arrogance of adolescence was sprinkled through what they had to say.

I don't mind my mother's company, but I prefer to be on my own. I talk to her quite a lot on many subjects, not just one specific one. I don't really go out with my mum anywhere. I do give her lifts . . . when I'm available. (age 17, mother 'data processor')

'Nags' was the most common criticism that boys made of their mothers and the context revealed how domestic chores could play a negative as well as a positive role. Bittman's research demonstrated how little teenage sons did around the house, proving yet again that mothers continued to bear most of the domestic responsibility whether they were home full-time or not. Women's resentment of this disproportionate burden is also well-documented.[58] But male people of any age still tended to put faith in the motherhood ideology rather than the evidence of their own eyes: more than one teenage son pronounced with the same absolute certainty as his father's generation: 'She likes doing it'.

Psychologist and social commentator Bettina Arndt coined the term 'exploding mum' to summarise the image of their mothers which a group of schoolboys conveyed to her.[59] The same pattern was apparent here: outbursts of maternal fury which, to the boys, were totally unexpected and unwarranted because they did not hear what must have been an extensive lead-up. At most, some gave the impression that an angry maternal wasp occasionally buzzed in the background of their consciousness. Exactly as their sisters claimed, they were not seriously heeding their mothers. The sudden eruption of a woman driven to the end of her tether startled them. They experienced her rage as: 'gets angry for no reason'. They did not like it at all. And, like their fathers before them, they translated female anger into 'nagging'. It was the most blatant example in this generation of masculinity defeating empathy.

Very few boys were harbouring deep resentments or long-running grievances against their mothers. According to them, the disputes were short, noisy outbursts. There was no sign that they left any scars—on the sons. In most cases, communication continued despite the arguments. One fourteen-year-old boy answered the question about whether or not he enjoyed his mother's company with the blunt monosyllable 'no', but he was unusual. More typical was the slightly aggressive 'And who wants to know?' tone, in the answer from another boy who, at fifteen, was right in the middle of his teens.

> *I talk to my mother because I like to, not out of duty. We both talk about everyday things. Some conversations are quite deep and meaningful, but never really deep (e.g. about sex, my relationship with my girlfriend, which my friends and I talk about). We have a good son–mother relationship.*

Occasionally, domestic chores could be detected playing their potentially, but all too rare, positive role as a vehicle for communication rather than argument. One eighteen-year-old nominated washing and shopping as among the everyday things that he did with his mother, but specially mentioned: 'the things we do together are talk and cook'.

Little evidence was apparent of mothers displaying the rigid attitudes and dogmatically-held opinions which so infuriated sons three decades ago. When it did occur, the boys resented this trait as much as their predecessors: [the worst is] . . . 'when she's cranky or when she's narrow-minded and won't listen'; 'her stubbornness about what she believes'; 'she always thinks she's right, all the time'. The small percentage who described this once familiar behaviour pattern were offset by an equally small percentage whose descriptions of their mothers went well beyond any maternal stereotype. Several of the younger generation plainly trusted their mother's judgment and valued her advice on subjects beyond her maternal role to an extent unimaginable thirty years earlier. 'Intelligent', 'wise', 'gives her opinion then leaves it to us', commented three 20-year-olds. 'Intelligent and smart', declared an adolescent aged fifteen.

The sons aged between twenty and thirty, who participated in this project mostly lived away from home either at college or in their own apartments. Those aged between eighteen and nineteen years had all either just left home or were about to do so. Although many had girlfriends and some lived with them, none under thirty were married. All the younger teenagers lived at home. It is true to say that the emotional bond with their mothers had not yet been tested but these sons differed from their fathers in being relaxed and unselfconscious in their mother's company at an age when many of the older men would have found her an embarrassing encumbrance.

Some confirmed their mother's claim that the ties between them could survive separation and an independent life. One young man spent most of his childhood alone with his very young single mother. Now, she was remarried and he lived in his own flat. She described their relationship as 'almost brother and sister' and his affectionate comments confirmed her point of view.

> *I do enjoy my mother's company because we don't get to spend a great deal of time together and when we do, we talk and talk about new things we have done, or what has been going on since we last saw each other. And she always asks me if I've got a girlfriend or not! (age 23)*

Many sons agreed with the mothers' opinion that the relationship opened up with particular richness as they began to move away from school and into adult life. Anything and everything could then be open to discussion with their mothers and, like the women, some described an amazing degree of frankness:

> *As for what we talk about, there's nothing we can't! Sex, drugs, politics, relationships, spirituality (although I'm growing cynical in that area.) I think one of the most off-putting things (to others) about us is our openness, always honest, too honest, blunt, straight to the point, hide nothing. But, in the end, I think it's a good attribute and, with age, I will get a better grip on its uses. I surely picked that one up from Mum. (age 21)*

There appeared to be resilience and flexibility in these mother–son friendships which could transcend different adult interests. Young men from varied backgrounds made it plain that they found their mothers good companions who were valued for their open minds, their tolerance and their ability to listen. There was virtually no sign of the frequent comments made by the previous generation about narrowness, the need to keep things secret from mothers, or mothers' inability to give appropriate advice. Better educated, more confident and worldly than previous generations, these mothers could talk to their sons more on their own terms. Their views were sought with the confidence that they could be discussed, queried or even disregarded without offence. Spared the heavy masculine conditioning of their fathers, these sons could more easily turn to their mothers as a sensitive and trustworthy confidante which the conventions of their masculine world denied them. A boy could be a poet and not lose face with his mother. He could also be just plain comfortable, finding in her company a refuge from striving to stay on top.

12 Mothers and daughters-in-law

The degree to which mothers and sons are governed by the male culture becomes more blatant as the sons' mature. 'Man' created the mother-in-law stereotype just as his ideas shaped the interaction between his wife and his mother, defining their relationship by an egotism which conceives people and events only in terms of itself. The difficulties that mothers and daughters-in-law experience will not be vanquished until they demolish these male rules and set their own.

Women adopt the masculine philosophies as their own. Almost without realising it, they come to mothering with ready-made expectations about what raising a boy involves. No mother of a son is unaware of the old jingle: 'Your son is a son till he takes a wife; your daughter's a daughter the rest of her life'. On the rare occasion that a woman is ignorant of this ditty, another woman will almost certainly take it upon herself to pass it on. Today's young mothers are receiving the old advice as surely as previous generations.

> *One of the main reasons I was disappointed when my babies were both boys was because when they're older and married the daughters-in-law are never as close to the mother-in-law and you never have that relationship to the grandchildren that you do through a daughter. Everyone's told me that, from older people right through to my own friends. And it's my own experience, I'm not close to my mother-in-law . . . When the boys marry, they'll drift away. (age 35)*

The process of 'letting *him* go' is often expressed as 'taking second place'. It was a common phrase in previous generations and, among the mothers who contributed to this book, it was explicitly used by several older women, sometimes prosaically, sometimes with self-denigrating humility. Others romanticised their loss in the terms that men defined for them, as a noble and emotional sacrifice. Only a very few retained their own dignity while accepting the simple principle that a young couple's first responsibility, of necessity, must be to each other. Even this idea was too often expressed as a matter of 'loyalty' to one woman or the other. The very phraseology associated with mothers and daughters-in-law has connotations ripe for conflict. 'Taking second place' almost creates resentment by itself. Displaced? Replaced? No longer first? Taking second place to whom? Another woman. In the saga of male–female relations, nowhere does 'divide and conquer' emerge as a more blatant scenario.

Mothers of sons have fought their harsh sentence surreptitiously. Even today, men are largely ignorant of how their carefully logical, masculine theory is white-anted from within. Long ago, women made a small but vital adjustment to the philosophy of 'letting go'. Diluting the male ideal with female pragmatism, they translated the grand sacrifice into the more domestically cosy notion of 'handing over'.

This idea of 'handing over' a son still exists. And it is not simply a matter of different terminology to describe the same process. 'Handing over' has different connotations than letting go or taking second place. Men may think it simply means that someone else will do their chores, but that was only ever symbolic and it has been the first aspect to fall into disrepute because younger Western women no longer expect to take care of their partners in this way. The term always had a maternal implication beyond physical nurturing. To women, it meant that an incomplete or immature person was 'handed over' by his mother to another woman not as a romantic rival, but as another mother who would 'finish him off'. Traditionally, they left room for the younger women to shape the male object to suit themselves. Some still do.

> *. . . wives play an important part in moulding husbands to their requirements, but I feel that the groundwork has to be done carefully by mothers for them [the sons] to respond. [age 58]*

A younger woman put it in more modern language but expressed exactly the same view.

> *They are both still at home, reliant upon 'Mum'. But I feel they will shape up well.* The modern girls will see that they do. *(Emphasis added) (age 54, sons 22 and 16)*

And in the popular press, a young woman talking about a failed relationship revealed that she had absorbed the same old message: 'From the time they are young, women are told, "you'll find a man and fix him up"'.[60]

In 1992, sociologist David de Vaus investigated the different ways in which parents of both sexes 'let go' of their children and the type of relationships which later existed in adult life. Although he did not describe it in those terms, he found evidence of the maternal pattern of 'handing over' an immature man. This valuable research revealed that, contrary to legend, mothers 'let go' of sons and daughters in similar numbers and in much the same manner. It revealed that they also hold on to their children of either sex to a similar extent, *but* they hold on differently.[61] It is in this difference that de Vaus' findings support the thrust of the argument mounted here. De Vaus designated one major category of unseparated mother–son relationships as being 'child-centred' because the child was the focus of attention and the parent's life was marginal. He found that 35 per cent of mothers related to their adult sons in this way compared to only 19 per cent of daughters. De Vaus assessed mothers in these 'child-centred' relationships as being unable to give up their maternal role because they need to be needed and involved. He noted that this behaviour fitted, in some respects, with Freud's theory that mothers compensate for not being male by holding on to and living through their sons. But this reiterates Freud's viewpoint, which was male.[62] A female observer might well detect evidence of the 'unfinished' child, the one who was still immature when his mother handed him on and who, she believes, continues to need her help. The end result is the same but the rationale is entirely, and significantly, different.

The (usually unspoken) female agreement about handing over from one to the other may have been workable so long as women were content to mother their men in exchange for security, but contemporary women increasingly seek adult partners to whom they can relate on equal terms. They will no longer tolerate living with a child masquerading as a man.

There was little evidence that mothers have addressed the implications of passing on male children who were physically and occupationally ready, but emotionally 'unfinished'. It appeared more as though they push this question aside in order to enjoy their own relationship with the boy before they 'lose' him. Women's much-touted empathy fails them on the subject of their sons' future relationships. With peculiar insensitivity, they seem unable to guess how their daughters-in-law might be feeling about them—or even see the need to take it into account. The comments of two modern mothers about their sons' relationship with girlfriends, posed crucial questions to an onlooker which neither woman had thought to ask herself. How did the girlfriends feel as they adjusted to their partner's style? What did they think about his mother?

> *He is now changing to a much more caring and sharing person . . . this can be attributed to the courtship of a wonderful young lady. (mother 44, son 21)*

> *I hope my son will always place his love above his mother. To date, he has expected his girlfriends to replace his mother and each time, she has fallen happily into the 'carer' role—maybe not so happily, but prepared to do it to remain his girlfriend. (mother 39, son 19)*

The stage is set for the encounter between mothers and their 'replacement'. Initially, daughters-in-law appear to blame their partner's mother mercilessly for the son's faults but, in the context of the long female tradition of 'handing over', their attitude becomes more explicable. In fact, they are holding her responsible for the man she passed on to them.

Mothers are very conscious that they must get on with their daughter-in-law or risk their entire relationship with their son. Desperate to avoid upsetting someone who might become permanent in his life, they prepare themselves to welcome whomever he chooses. Most are extremely cautious about expressing any opinion about her.

> *With all my children I tread carefully where I might intrude . . . In the area of my son's relationships, I say very little for fear of offending. I can honestly say I have never felt jealous of his female friends. They are always made welcome in our home and there has usually been good rapport. It would make me very sad if his partner felt the need to cut me out of his life, since I can't see that I would be any sort of threat. I would be very sad to lose him in any way. I hope his wife will share him with me. (age 53)*

The phrase 'share him' recurs among mothers' comments about their sons' relationships with women. Scared of being too possessive, most are looking to share and are hoping that they can do their part to make it possible. Good intentions to share rather than fight, however, do not always survive in the long term. One mother proudly described how she did not feel at all jealous when her son first brought home a girlfriend, yet she subsequently related a bitter battle with her daughter-in-law in which the antagonism arose from her own refusal to stop mothering him.

Traditionally, mothers headed off girls that they did not like. They made their feelings known obliquely by throwaway remarks, or a stiff manner which the son, and usually the girlfriend too, could detect. It is unlikely that this tactic has entirely vanished, although the current generation of mothers is trying particularly hard to be impartial.

Older sons with some experience of introducing girlfriends to their mother reckoned that they always knew what she thought. Even if she said nothing directly, there would be comments: 'I don't like her eyes', 'Diana, the huntress'. These middle-aged men dismissed their mother's opinions as irrelevant, most denying that she had any effective influence and one emphasising how he went ahead despite his mother's open disapproval. A few conceded that a mother's reaction had swayed their attitude in relation to girlfriends, if not to choice of wife. 'She was particularly attracted to girls who didn't have mothers. I think she liked to mother them.'

None of the younger sons saw their mother as influencing their choice of girlfriend although some acknowledged the value of her general advice about all things female. One teenager had been aware of his girlfriend's insecurity around his mother and explained it by drawing the specific comparisons which every girlfriend dreads and imagines must occur all the time.

> *I have just ended a relationship. My ex-girlfriend felt threatened by Mum. I sensed it every time they met. Intelligence gap! (age 19)*

Girlfriends are insecure about a boy's mother even when she does nothing. More confident and experienced than they, closer to their boyfriend, who loves her with a certainty they want for themselves, she makes them feel inadequate just by existing. This attitude is aggravated because, even today, young girls have not been reared with the idea that young men can love more than one woman at once. For too many, it is still a competition. They cannot share. They must replace.

When describing their own emotions, the younger sons incidentally revealed the way in which their girlfriends' attitudes began to affect the mother–son relationship and most of the boys admitted to divided loyalties. Given that many were in the transition phase between the end of adolescence and their early twenties, this tug of feeling is not surprising. Indeed, their honest admission is reassuring that, unlike their fathers' generation, they feel no conditioned imperative to deny it. Of real concern, however, was the evidence that it was the girlfriends' lack of confidence which created the divided loyalty. The younger women were already sowing seeds of dissent, denigrating the mother's opinions, or being reluctant to visit her. One twenty-year-old girl even produced the 'mummy's boy danger' as a reason why her boyfriend should move out of home. If the son is already in conflict with his mother, these ideas fall on fertile ground for then the romantic female tactic of 'playing up who he wants her to be' comes into operation and the alliance between the two young people can lay the basis for a lasting relationship. In the past, heavy masculine conditioning predisposed sons to believe that they were not supposed to love both women simultaneously and encouraged them to reject any suggestion of 'undue' attachment to their mothers. But a majority of contemporary sons, at eighteen to twenty-two years, had a positive relationship with their mother which they were not prepared simply to jettison. For them tension was not always the result of ill-feeling. It could also arise just from the son's love for both parties. Whatever its source, the younger men were caught in the same tug-of-war that their fathers experienced, but perhaps with more commitment to finding an equipoise between their affections for both women.

> *I never get caught between obligations with my girlfriend and my Mum. They are both totally different in my heart and mind. My girlfriend likes my mother, although she thinks she is rather 'I want my children to have the best' all the time . . . And she also thinks it's silly that my mother wants to mould us into something that, maybe, we're just not cut out to be. But my partner respects Mum a*

great deal and is always worried what she will think of her. (age 20)

My girlfriend gets on well with my mother—they always have plenty to talk about, although my girlfriend generally does not look forward to meeting her as it requires quite an effort. I do feel caught between obligations to my parents and my girlfriend. The parents do not complain audibly, though my mother would be the one to do so, if either did. (age 24)

There seems to be no jealousy or rivalry. My girlfriend acts like a daughter . . . she will often talk things through with Mum. When we are not at college together, my girlfriend and I live about 100 miles apart and, naturally, I often go up to see her. Almost equally as often . . . I feel torn between the two. Half of me wants to stay here, the other to go. It is easier when I am away from home and, ultimately, at its most comfortable when both are here at the same time. (age 22)

Mostly, mothers are right or at least wise, not to risk saying what they think. They have too much to lose. The sons' view about whether or not their mothers should offer an opinion was, however, by no means unanimous, although whether they were always fair to their mothers on this issue was sometimes questionable. One of the older men still carried traces of resentment that his mother had 'let him' marry disastrously without uttering a warning. It had taken many years before he could appreciate why she did not say anything, but his sense of betrayal lingered despite the rationalisations. Decades later, he continued to misinterpret what was almost certainly meant as reassurance that he had made the right decision. His eventual reinterpretation that she had the right maternal attitude to independence, still missed her attempt to comfort him.

I finally decided to break the relationship and when I told my mother, she said: 'I knew it wasn't going to work. She was a nice girl, but you're much better off without her'. And I thought to myself, Well, why didn't you tell me three years ago. Now, of course, I realise the value of allowing me to make my own decisions. (age 53)

Another much younger man was equally surprised by how well

his mother had hidden her doubts. His story is a small but significant indicator of both the changing nature of the relationship between mothers and sons and the loosening gender constrictions on men. His mother's behaviour was very like her predecessors. Her overall answer revealed her reluctance to interfere, but her son felt far less obliged than his father's generation had done to be self-reliant and independent in every circumstance. He valued his mother's judgment across a wide range of issues and felt comfortable in seeking reassurance that he was making the right decision. Although he asked her opinion at the time when he broke his engagement, he was amazed some years later, to discover the depth of her feelings.

> *In retrospect I can see the hesitation, but I thought it was a bit of jealousy because some of my affection was taken away. My sister told me only recently that Mum had 'bad vibes' from the beginning. Mum told her: 'I can't talk to Laura as I'd like to. She doesn't seem to click with me. But she's his choice and I guess I'll have to make the effort'. She had all these doubts and she didn't express them. When I was going through the trauma of deciding to end it, I really needed someone to validate my decision and I contacted my mother. Only after I'd expressed my doubts, did she say, 'Yes, well, I agree with that'. And she was very helpful. I felt very relieved afterwards. (age 30)*

The three-way dynamics established at the beginning are remarkably persistent. Few men or women described a relationship which had changed much along the way. If a son's partner told him that his mother thought that she was 'not good enough', the man's response was usually to try and convince her that she was wrong. Wives could be caught in a very difficult position. Sometimes, their mothers-in-law were running a hidden agenda which only they saw. And their husbands were no help, mostly oblivious to the problem or preferring to dismiss it as trivial. Talking about this subject, men could contradict themselves between one sentence and the next without noticing the inconsistency. One minute a man might claim that his wife was imagining that his mother did not like her yet, shortly after, unconsciously reveal that the younger woman's perception had been accurate: his mother had been disappointed, or doubtful, or perhaps jealous, of his choice. And he knew it. The male inability to empathise was sometimes very obvious. Even if a man appreciated the difficulty with his mind, he could not imagine how it hurt. And, once a disapproving or resentful tension had been established between the women, it could continue for decades, even though the mother never made a single direct comment, even though the wife was always welcoming and the son, nonchalant.

Cultural or religious differences have always aggravated the relationship between mothers and their daughters-in-law, but the transformation in women's lifestyle and ambitions since the 1960s has created the biggest gulf between female generations. There are many new reasons for ill-feeling. Once, the health and behaviour of the children, the standard of housework or the cooking were the main targets for criticism, just as they could also form a bond between two women. Today, the matter of working wives and mothers complicates this traditional agenda. The subjects which could once be links are more likely to divide than bind. The older women hold strong opinions. In fact, it may be the only area in which they are really confident of their judgment since it was their equivalent to a career. They see only the worldly veneer of their daughters-in-law and overestimate their self-confidence. Both generations are striving to emulate the 'perfect mother', so criticism from the older woman on this issue is almost guaranteed to trigger wracking guilt in the younger woman which her mother-in-law is unaware she has caused. And there is another trap for the mother-in-law. A wife may fight with her own mother about differences in their lifestyle, but comments from her husband's mother risk aggravating tension between husband and wife on the same subject. If they are already fighting about it, a daughter-in-law will immediately classify his mother as 'interfering' or 'thinks he can do no wrong' rather than a fairer response of 'entitled to her opinion'.

Mothers-in-law are not always victimised. Some refuse to concede ground to another woman's different approach and behave appallingly. Lack of respect for difference, lack of imagination to appreciate the intrusion which their stubborn opinions represent and the distress they cause to a much younger woman, too often demonstrate exactly the behaviour which has given mothers-in-law a bad name. It cannot be blamed on male disparagement, or ill-will from a daughter-in-law, but is very much a woman's own responsibility. The older women have Hobson's choice in their relationships with their daughters-in-law. They are just as easily condemned for doing nothing as for doing too much. They worry about how to establish a relationship with their son's partner, but ultimately have very little influence on how it evolves—except, maybe, those for whom fear of loss outweighs their son's happiness, making them cling on and drive away the girlfriend. For most mothers, this is not an option. They let their child go even at their own expense.

The degree to which a man's mother will have a place in his adult life is very much affected by the daughter-in-law's attitude. Author Leila Friedman discovered the potential tragedy which lies in wait for the mother of a son. Although her subject was how grandparents were affected by their children's divorce, she amassed much information about mothers and daughters-in-law.

> There were a lot of women cut off from their grandchildren because their mother thought that *her* mother was the only true grandmother . . . One widow lost her only son because his wife's parents, both police force, told her that he was the image of their own son who died as a teenager and they regarded him not as a son-in-law, but as a substitute son. The son was too weak to fight three strong-minded people and would not see or speak to his mother. I just had to tell her to put her love on hold and hope the marriage would eventually fail, but she died of a heart attack a year later. I don't think she wanted to live any longer.[63]

This situation is the secret dread of every mother of a son. It lies behind the joyful celebration of the relationship even for a younger generation of mothers. Author and journalist Geraldine Taylor stumbled on this carefully hidden maternal grief when, to her surprise, she experienced it herself. Only forty-six, with a stimulating career and a supportive husband, she had not anticipated any great difficulty.

> *I didn't expect to feel any different when my son left for university—in fact, I'd never given my feelings much thought. I tend not to. The day he left, it was as though I was taken over by*

> *something outside myself—my heart pounded. I felt awful panic and I just walked and walked. About 12 miles. I think the feeling is insecurity and fear—I felt as though it was the end of things—the end of all the happiness we'd had. And insecurity because I knew I could never ask for the reassurance that it wasn't the end. I realised I had a personal fight on my hands when I found myself saying 'When Peter was alive . . .'. Then, I could see the extent of my sadness. It took eight months of hard mental struggle and walking hundreds of miles to feel strong and in control again and to feel less insecure. It is a grief and one which I had to fight very hard . . . My husband was badly affected too. We became very possessive of each other and had to make an effort to get back to our normal, independent selves . . . It's not as though it is all over. I can understand that now. But it is hard to see what part a mum can play in her adult son's life. I just need to feel I'll always have some place in his heart.*[64]

Curious to discover whether her feeling was shared by others, Taylor extended her personal experience into professional research. In mid-1992 she interviewed twenty-five mothers, aged in their early forties and early fifties. Their sons, generally around twenty years old, had all left home. Nine of the women were mothers of only sons but sixteen had other children. Twenty-three of them suffered the kind of devastation Taylor herself experienced. Some resorted to bizarre attempts to alleviate their sense of loss. Others bought pets as emotional compensation and this seemed to help their husbands too. Taylor reported that predominant among their feelings was 'the fear that there will be no place in his life for them'. A fifty-year-old mother who was also a teacher asked in bewildered sorrow:

> *What is possible now? What can I expect? I'm OK. I couldn't tell him, or my family, how I feel. I talk about it with some of my friends who feel the same. That helps. I expect I'll get over it. What I need is to know where we go from here.*[65]

These women cannot be dismissed as examples of some notorious maternal stereotype. Although Taylor commented that some were 'a little in love with their sons', they were not women without other interests or other children, who did not know how to separate from their boys. Many had other occupations as well as being a mother. Most had other children. One woman with two sons still at home wept for the one who had gone: 'If I'd known it would be like this, all this pain, I'd never have had children at all'. A few of the mothers who talked to Taylor were single parents, but most had husbands. In some cases, the men shared their grief.[66] This was not the 'normal' sorrow which mothers can expect as their children leave home. It was a more focused unhappiness, exacerbated by uncertainty, fear and the need to conceal it. Taylor reported that it related specifically to sons. Mothers of daughters who had left home (or who have both sons and daughters) were quick to point out that it is not the same with girls. They told her that daughters remain in closer contact and can be anticipated to be friends for life. Most of the women who spoke to Taylor saw no alternative to keeping their feelings a secret. They feared the embarrassment both to their sons and their families. Tragically, they also feared that if they expressed the need for more affection, they might get less.[67] Mothers grieve because, deep down, they see through the pretence about mothers and sons. However close and affectionate the relationship has been, they realise that the culture will encourage their sons to discard them. Instructed to 'let go', they know that the psychologically authorised interpretation actually means 'rejection'. It is this context which creates their grief, not the failure of an individual mother, nor, for that matter, of an individual son.

Germaine Greer said on television in 1991 that 'to be a mother is to have no claim on anyone'.[68] Most women who took part in this book expressed opinions which agreed with Greer. To a woman, they said that their sons had 'no obligation' to them. Equally, they believed that they, as mothers, had no rights. There was no evidence that they were conscious that Greer's subsequent qualification might apply to them: '. . . but, on the other hand, your name will be invoked whenever there's a difficulty'.[69] Presumably, that was someone else's mother, the 'typical' mother.

When the sons were asked whether they felt that they had any ongoing obligation to their mother a small generational shift did become apparent. The few middle-aged men who admitted any obligation at all interpreted it as a practical one, such as financial assistance or help with shopping. A number of sons from both generations expressed the traditional idea that they must live up to their mothers' expectations of academic or career success. The notable change was a sparse trend among the youngest sons to interpret 'obligation' as meaning that they had an emotional responsibility to play a part in sustaining the relationship with their mother. And, unlike the older generation, they showed no sign that they felt keeping in touch conferred any favour. Their mothers had apparently succeeded in 'sacrificing' but not abnegating themselves. By contrast, a woman from an earlier era had lived up to an ideal of motherhood too well.

> *She puts no obligation on me . . . I ring her whenever I feel like it. If it's two weeks, she's grateful. If it's one hour, she's grateful. Three months, she's grateful. Any contact I make with her is a bonus.*

It is too early to judge what rewards or disappointments the younger women will reap for having been the mothers of sons, but the verdict is already underway for the older generation. There are few kisses. 'I no longer kiss Mum. It's only a simple thing, but as a symbol I think it's important.' Much chauvinism under other names, such as competent, masterful and dominant: '. . . he is patronising, always trying to gain the upper hand . . .'. And little comfort according to a grievance counsellor who works with bereaved widows:

> Sons come and tell their mothers what to do and when to stop grieving. Daughters are more considerate for longer although neither will allow the full range of grief unless someone points out that it's normal. But the sons are really heavy. Very heavy indeed. There's hardly any 'give', no understanding that their mother is on her own after maybe forty years. Many of the sons have been virtually out of contact since they left home . . . their children are the link back to mother. The son assumes he will take charge and his mother will do what he bids and let him get back to his wife.[70]

Few wives revealed enough empathy for their mother-in-law to take account of this kind of tragedy. They are predisposed to encounter a possessive, interfering woman who will take her son's side in arguments and cause rifts with his partner. Always very conscious of the 'not good enough' legend, the insecurity of daughters-in-laws can help the myth become reality, even when it has no foundation. They are alert to the slightest sign of disapproval or disappointment. Whether real or imagined, if they detect even a trace, battle will be joined. And there are more fundamental issues than domestic chores to hold against a mother. The alliance which begins when a girlfriend sympathises with a boy about his mother can deepen into real anger on her man's behalf when, as a wife, she gradually discovers the scars he bears from the relationship. If they come as a surprise, or a disappointment, then her anger is all the greater for being mixed with resentment that she must live with the result of such damaging child-rearing.

Daughters-in-law hold mothers responsible for the man's faults. In particular, they blame her if he cannot express emotion. In the context of their own marriage, they forget the idea of 'handing on' even when they share it, which most do. Instead of sympathetic understanding, they bitterly resent their partner's mother for failing to raise an emotionally mature man who can take responsibility for himself. The bond of rueful tolerance which past generations of women so often shared towards these child–men has almost vanished. Modern women, whose love cannot survive the disillusionment of being married to one, seek a divorce.

> *My ex-husband was the last child after three daughters and he was the 'apple of his mother's eye'. Every family member had to jump to his attention. To this day, 42 years later, he will consult his mother and father on decisions he should make himself. The whole eight years we were married, he* always *consulted Mum, half the time not even speaking to me on these matters. As the saying goes, 'They never grow up'. This is quite right in his case. (age 41)*

Stereotyped expectations about the sexes play a major part in the ill-feeling between mother and daughter-in-law. One of the most misleading, yet notorious, problems is the mother who truly does think that her son 'can do no wrong'. She is always regarded as someone with a personal problem but most women who romanticise men, including their own sons as men, invariably over-rate the whole male sex and undervalue other women. They are far more likely to be critical of their son's partner, blaming her for everything, while absolving him totally of responsibility. One wife had become the target of all of the female members of her husband's family, even when she supported him while he chopped and changed jobs, always failing from his own efforts but always blaming everyone else. His mother and her daughters had a litany of excuses for his behaviour and saw nothing admirable at all in his wife's efforts.

Among the contributions from more than 150 mothers, a pattern of 'blame the female and spare the male' was evident across several cultures and between generations. It was the ultimate extension of women's failure to hold their sons responsible as boys for their actions and their emotions. Consequently, the notable absentees from the infamous female battleground are its objects of dispute—the men. Some of the men choose to be bystanders; some disregard any tension or are entirely oblivious to it. Whichever position they adopt, they do so because the women who love them allow it. In most cases, neither wife nor mother treat the man in the middle as an active participant in the triangle of their relationship.

There was some evidence of wives doing their best to improve a bad relationship between mother and son, but it was infrequent. Mostly, their attitude reflected that of their husbands. If a son valued his mother and dealt kindly with her, the two women in his life more easily overcame any difficulties between themselves. Good relationships developed even quicker when a daughter-in-law either had no mother or was alienated from her own. Some mothers-in-law foresaw the potential and encouraged their son to marry a girl who was motherless. Then they adopted her, gaining a daughter rather than losing a son. The comparative success of this type of relationship illuminated how 'interfering' mothers must frequently be motivated by fear of exclusion rather than by the legendary possessiveness. The younger woman's attitude is also different. She is less critical and more ready to value her mother-in-law.

> *. . . my husband is attentive and loves his mother, but I don't think he enjoys her company as I do. My own mother died soon*

after our marriage and she told me, 'I know I can't replace your mother, but I would like to be a mother to you and I'd like you to think of me in that way'. And I have, to a large extent. She is a lovely person, eighty-one years old now and very active. She likes coming out with me for lunch etc., although mostly I visit her. So far, I don't have to assist her. She shares her worries with me, which I am pleased about. However, she must surely enjoy the company of her elder son more than that of his wife, yet she sees less of him because he is at work, or we are away on our boat. (age 54)

Feminism was a positive influence at all stages of the mother–daughter-in-law relationship because it broke down stereotypes. Female fellowship and more understanding of women's situation predisposed the two generations to appreciate and respect each other as much for their differences as for any shared interests. Competition for the son was replaced by a three-way relationship which was differentiated on an individual basis rather than by roles. Mothers who were feminists frequently established friendships with their sons' girlfriends which survived in their own right even after the younger women's relationship with their son had ended. Without exception, any wife who was prepared to declare herself a feminist subsequently found something positive to say about her mother-in-law even when the relationship contained the same elements which so enraged other women.

My husband was a good son, tender, loving, concerned and helpful, but his mother did make it easy for him. He was an only boy, the youngest and her 'golden-haired one who could do no wrong'. How he ever grew up to be as sensitive and thoughtful to others with all the adulation, I'll never know. They did have a comradeship between them, a shared sense of humour which probably helped to keep him level-headed. How did I feel about her? I guess I resented the fact that she could see no wrong in him when, despite all his good points, he is at least as human as I am with pluses and minuses mixed up. His mother and I were friends all along, but probably 'guarded' friends. (age fifties)

My husband and his mother share a special bond developed over years with a difficult and domineering father–husband. My husband's father was not violent or unpleasant, but did not allow for different opinions to his own. My mother-in-law is a very intelligent woman. She did not achieve her full potential due to a non-supportive father, post-war discrimination in further education, and her husband. All her ambitions have been sublimated to his. I like and admire her greatly. (age 28)

Feminist mothers were more likely to make allowances for the different context of the older women's lives and its effect on their attitudes. Belief in feminism probably also made the younger women more confident of their lifestyle and its choices. Some were full-time mothers. Some worked. Because the latter regarded their work as important, they did not feel guilty about it and, significantly, could not easily be *made* to feel guilty by someone else.

Ultimately, the solution to the troubled mother–daughter-in-law relationship lies in individual human beings. At present, it is not something of which women can be proud. Men may set the parameters but, as if mindlessly programmed, women fight. The rights and wrongs vary from one case to the next: sometimes the mother may be justified, sometimes the wife. It is largely irrelevant. In the wider context, neither are particularly admirable. And all women share their shame. Compassion is frequently displaced by triumph. There is too much ready criticism, too little generosity or kindness or understanding. Almost no empathy. Too often, one woman is hurting another, when both are the mothers of sons. Only three or four made this connection in a way which affected their own behaviour. One of them was the mother of an eight-year-old boy.

I shall no doubt find it difficult to accept another woman in his life. I now appreciate how my mother-in-law feels and I sympathise to some extent because I 'have' her son. My husband is not very good as a son. He contacts his parents very little, just when he feels he ought to, like birthdays, Christmas etc. He doesn't contact them just out of interest or the desire to talk, like I do with my parents. I find his mother very bossy, but I think it must be hard for her as he doesn't keep close to her. I try to allow her time with him when we do all get together as she must really value these moments. (age 39)

'Time together' is all most mothers would ask—some time alone to continue the adult version of a relationship which was once so important in both their lives. Sadly, they are often reliant on a daughter-in-law's generosity to make it possible. It is a reflection on both women that such consideration is notable by its absence. They need to trust and respect each other, stop blaming or undermining each other and hold the man in the middle responsible for his actions and his feelings.

13 Signposts to the future

Before the 1960s, there was no shortage of information about how to raise boys. Instructions emanated from church and community regarding the character and responsibilities required of a man. Fathers too, made their strong views known. Boys must be tough. They must not cry. Above all, they must not be 'sissies'. Mothers usually smothered any personal doubts and deferred to male opinion. The popular media provided another authoritative source of advice, endlessly recycling Freudian-based theories, conveying discreetly-phrased warnings about a mother's potential to damage her boy's sexual identity. Women of all ages during that period absorbed the risk of being 'too seductive', 'too possessive', 'too protective', too . . . too . . . too . . . !' So, mothers kept their distance. And they were careful with their kisses. Conscious of the boy's role in society, they did their best to prepare him in an appropriately masculine fashion. In the process, his individual nature could be overlooked. At worst, it could be ruthlessly pummelled into a veneer which fitted the community's masculine standard.

The onset of feminism put mothers and daughters on the agenda for the first time, sidelining mothers and sons for what has, so far, proved to be a very long time. This displacement had an unforeseen consequence. While mothers' approach to raising daughters changed, the theories and strictures about sons were left to flourish virtually unchallenged. One of the marked continuities in the relationship was how the Freudian views so prevalent in the 1950s still influenced mothers' attitudes in the 1990s.

Another continuity, and one which transcended all others in importance, was self-esteem—not the child's but the mother's. Feminists have documented only too well how a mother's lack of self-esteem is internalised by her daughter and acts to limit the child's confidence, constraining her aspirations and achievements. Feminists assumed that sons, being a different sex, escaped the ill-effects of their mothers' effacement. The more extreme among them declared that while daughters wanted 'courageous mothering', boys 'demanded' sacrificial mother love.[71] Such a case may be sustained at an abstract, philosophical level, but in personal terms it is expedient and wrong. Sons are affected as detrimentally as daughters, but in different ways. Not only does it shape their general expectation of how women will relate to them, it also poisons their individual relationship with their mothers. The sons of the post-war decades longed for their mothers to express their needs, to get angry, to disagree, not to be a walkover, but to stand up to them so that they could respect and like where they already loved. Those with mothers who could not challenge them in this way experienced anguish and ambivalence. They might have taken the women's nurturing for granted, but not their lack of self-respect.

The ideology of motherhood offered both parties an escape. Mothers used it, as some still do, to avoid the anxieties learned in their own childhood relationships. It was an acceptable way to dodge conflict by making no demands and asserting no needs. Other mothers, who were driven by different anxieties, were empowered by motherhood to extract the obedience they craved as reassurance of their worth.[72] Many of these women harrassed their children to an extent which left the sons resentful at the difference between the 'ideal mother' and their own, and utterly bewildered by the later feminist notion that their mothers were downtrodden. The women's personal weakness exacerbated the hard reality of motherhood, making many strained and shrill as they struggled to exert a control which felt particularly unnatural with male children. With the stubborn rigidity born of lack of confidence, they clung to dogmatic or superficial opinions. Their sons did not detect their inner uncertainty but reacted to these qualities with miserable fury. Ideas about mothering disguised the truth. Motherhood made a virtue of female lack of self-esteem.

Contrary to feminist assumptions, the sons of this generation did not feel powerful or enhanced by their mothers' subordination. Either they experienced their mother as dominating by failing to see her precarious veneer, or they were exasperated by her subjugation and grasped the motherhood ideology gratefully, even desperately, as an explanation for it. But they believed the 'ideal' mother was a real mother. When theirs did not behave accordingly, they were bewildered and hurt. As middle-aged men, few could say that they loved their mother unequivocally; few could see her in context and discover compassion for her shortcomings. Many recalled a childhood devoid of affection and held their mothers responsible. As adults, most were uncomfortable, impatient and bored in the women's company.

These men did not 'blame' their mothers while excusing their fathers. In both generations, sons' judgment of their male parent was predominantly merciless. Only a minority aligned themselves emotionally with their fathers rather than their mothers—and only the teenagers still wept for the loss of their fathers. The older sons had buried the pain deep, many simply writing off the relationship in scathing terms. Significantly, only those sons without fathers believed in the paternal relationship along the lines of social legend. They yearned for the father they assumed other boys had—a masculine example who would fill an emotional vacuum in their own lives. In later years, it was these fatherless sons who were often the most determined to spend time and share interests with their own children.

Mothers' relationships with their sons were deeply affected by the relationship between the two males. In varying degrees, the women were the emotional conduit, the peacemaker, the promoter and the protector between them. Only the older women, the mothers of the 1950s, referred sentimentally to fathers as role models. Most younger women had begun by being romantically predisposed towards the boy's father as a role model, cherishing any signs of a good relationship between them, but most were ultimately disillusioned. Nevertheless, they did not challenge the importance of a male role model. In a father's absence, they searched out relatives or male friends as substitutes. Sons of all ages appraised their fathers' personal qualities harshly and rejected the possibility of being like them. Their reaction was not a product of feminism, or divorce, although both were influential. This view was as prevalent among the middle-aged sons who grew up in the maritally stable 1950s as it was among the younger men and boys.

Attitudes to fathers remained substantially unchanged, but the discrepancy between mothers' and sons' opinion of each other reduced markedly in the younger generation. There was still much evidence of general male disparagement about mothers, but some of the younger boys asserted: 'There is no such thing as a typical mother'. Many sons still assumed that mothers should fit some 'good mother' yardstick and some of them still took refuge in the motherhood ideology to find something that they could praise, but they had less need to do so because the working mother offered them another way of judging her. Most boys who had this choice admired their mother for achievements unrelated to raising them. They could avoid the ambivalence of assessing her success in their own lives. Generally, sons found it much easier to admire mothers who worked, some of the youngest even regarding the women as people to emulate.

All ambiguities could be transcended by high self-esteem. In any era, a self-confident mother could surmount her circumstances. Her personality could defeat any fashionable ideology, whether maternal or feminist. A difficult authoritarian husband, the vulnerability of sole parenthood, the intimidation of masculinity, the ambivalent decision to mother full-time or to work, did not hinder a confident woman's relationship with her son. She did not need a job to affirm her worth. She did not need to cloak herself in motherhood to justify her choices, nor use its sentiments to disguise her fear of conflict. She could assert herself forthrightly and she could argue. She could retract or apologise, trust her judgment, admit her ignorance. These were the qualities which sons valued, in fact or in memory, throughout their lives. They had the same positive effect on the relationship with boys in the 1950s as they did in the following decades. Only the proportions who experienced it changed. The mother–son relationship has been a direct beneficiary of the widespread increase in women's self-esteem since the 1960s.

Women's education began the change. Feminism extended it. Betty Friedan was triggered into writing *The Feminine Mystique* by observing the malaise among college graduates who became full-time mothers in the 1950s. And it was tertiary-educated women in the 1960s who marshalled their intellectual capacity to conceptualise the feminist issues which turned a trickle of educated women into a flood. Throughout the 1970s, and ever since, the proportion of women seeking further education has steadily increased.

Comparisons between the comments of the post-war sons and the post-1960s sons immediately illuminates the benefit of equal education for women. The angry exasperation which sons felt for mothers who clung rigidly to dogma and simplistic ideas has vanished. The very qualities which the younger sons applaud are the ones that their fathers yearned for, predominantly the result of education: flexibility, open-mindedness, tolerance, abstract thought and intellectual curiosity. The younger generation is not bored or impatient in their mothers' company. Even at the height of adolescence, many take much pleasure in the women's friendship.

Feminism did the mother–son relationship some service by exposing women's inferior status and the way in which women internalised their oppression into a derogatory self-image. It also legitimised the affirmation of work outside the home. In other ways, feminists' actions were a direct contradiction to their goal of equality. Their views forced mothers to quarantine sons from the influence of feminism. Mothers of boys were left to consider feminist issues from an anti-male perspective. Many women offered their son a doll and were secretly relieved when he dropped it on its head to pick up a car or a mock weapon instead. It confirmed their suspicion that masculinity was innate. Most also found it delightful. In particular, it 'authorised' mother's relationship with sons to continue along the same lines it had always done.

Feminism empowered the female point of view and in general this benefited the mother–son relationship, giving mothers some much-needed confidence in their judgment. But the support feminism provided for the female perspective was not all positive. As psychologists point out, a mother's ability to understand her child's needs (and balance them with her own) is critical to the success of their relationship,[73] but feminism encouraged some mothers of sons to think that they did not need to understand the male point of view and this helped to perpetuate inequality.

The allegation that mothers were 'easier' on their sons became notorious in the 1970s as post-war daughters began to discuss their position in the family. Their brothers denied it vehemently. And, as middle-aged men, still do. The debate has continued unresolved, skimming the surface so that the fundamental difference in how mothers once related to sons is usually overlooked: although they prepared their daughters to do the 'emotional housework' for everyone, they failed to hold the boys emotionally responsible at all. Sons were reared to be responsible for everything, except themselves.

Comments by contemporary sisters revealed that the difference persists. Virtually all the teenage girls who took part in this study denied any favouritism existed. Their mothers had succeeded in making them feel as loved and valued as their brothers but, apparent in their answers, and all the more obvious because the girls were so confident that there was no favouritism, was how the notorious 'easier' treatment lay in the dynamics of the relationship. Daughters did not describe their brothers' excellent interaction with their mothers as 'flirting', they used words like 'jokey', 'teasing', 'laugh a lot'. They also described mothers who did not pursue discipline in the face of their sons' anger, or because the boys made them laugh. The girls compared their own relationship with their mothers as 'more mature', 'more responsible'. (The most accurate description is probably 'unsparing'.) They were content with the difference and even felt favoured by it. Most described their brothers affectionately, called them 'friends' and, if they did not exactly 'idolise', certainly held them in almost romanticised high regard. Simultaneously, they displayed the genesis of a rueful, virtually maternal tolerance for the boys' shortcomings which strongly resembled that of their mothers and held them no more responsible for themselves than the older women did.

Boys hesitate on the edge of what is happening but cannot quite come to grips with it. A few of the younger ones appeared to detect the difference in their mothers' relationship with their sisters. In an amorphous, undefined way, they sensed that they were missing out on something important, but their attempts to be part of it were usually dismissed as jealousy. A twelve-year-old boy made one of the shrewdest observations when he said: 'Mothers are easier on boys because they were girls and know what it is like'. He glimpsed how mothers can assess their daughters' emotional capacity more accurately and so dare to stretch it further. And some of the young men in their twenties, whose parents had divorced as they entered their teens, mentioned how it changed their relationship with their mothers and made them more mature. Any son who felt that he had been emotionally stretched to maturity was grateful for it.

Women's failure to hold sons emotionally responsible was starkly exposed by the interaction between mothers and daughters-in-law. Mothers described the grown men, who were their sons, as 'not allowed' to see them. Wives complained bitterly of their partners' shortcomings, particularly those who failed to take responsibility, yet they held the men's mothers responsible for this immaturity even into middle age. And the sons themselves rarely took the emotional initiative to settle the relationship with the two most important women in their lives. Researcher Leila Friedman found much evidence of men sneaking round to visit their mothers without telling their wives,[74] and other examples of daughters-in-law feeling obliged to 'break the bond' between mothers and sons when the real issue was not independence, but the man's level of emotional responsibility.

The quandary created for mothers and daughters-in-law is a continuation of the male rules which construct the mother–son relationship. Male culture wounds mothers and sons terribly in ways that neither understand. Men blame individual mothers for what is actually a cultural shortcoming. Women internalise an inferiority in this particular relationship which, although slightly modified in recent decades, continues fundamentally unchanged from forty years ago. They do not articulate the hurt and the loss of confidence which their sons' attitudes create. Instead, they disguise it, commenting with amusement on the quaint, loveable, innately masculine habits of little boys. But their behaviour is increasingly influenced not just by how they feel as mothers, but how they might come across to their boys as the 'typical mother of a son'. Most are intensely fearful that their son might experience them as the stereotypical mother: intrusive, dominating, cloying, over-emotional. The self-esteem which so many younger women gained in other aspects of contemporary life is always vulnerable in this old-fashioned relationship.

Women's romantic imagination about the nature of men

disguises the derogatory treatment which they often receive from their sons. It also blinds them to their own ignorance about the process of masculine conditioning, a discrepancy for which their sons suffer since it makes it difficult to comprehend the boys' real needs. The fundamental importance of physical and, equally, of verbal dominance in establishing a boy's relationship with his peers is underestimated. So is the devastating inadequacy which develops in boys who 'fail' to measure up to the masculine yardstick. The endless testing, the tension of constantly bracing for attack and the brittle shell which develops to hide a boy's vulnerability are all observed by women but their full significance is missed. Their failure to understand the male perspective can result in young sons feeling betrayed by mothers who are doing their best to be helpful.

The misinterpretation continues, unrecognised, into the adolescent years. There, it takes a different form. Like men, women confuse male sexuality with male social conditioning, believing the greater the masculinity, the more potent the male. They call the postures of masculinity 'showing off', 'childish', 'can't stop competing' with no idea how much of it is likely to be a defensive tactic against other males. And few mothers understand how the demands of being masculine in Western society steadily closes down boys' capacity for empathy, contradicting their own attempts to develop their boys' expressive side. Rather, they accept men's romantic presentation of masculinity as the accurate version. Some mothers are genuinely convinced that it is innately male to need less affection than females. Many interpret their own rejection as an expression of male emotional strength and self-sufficiency. Some men bear lasting scars inadvertently caused by their mother's stereotypical assumptions about males. A son could wonder endlessly why his mother did not intervene when he needed her or why she expected him to cope by himself. Men do not realise that women believe the legends about masculinity.

Sons had no idea of how masculinity affected them. They were equally unaware of the impact on their mothers. Only a few of the older men had been provoked by feminism into analysing male socialisation in the same way that women have analysed feminine conditioning. Those who did understand feminist issues were notably more compassionate towards their mothers even when the actual relationship had been bitter and hurtful. Most adult sons had no comprehension of the role of male culture in shaping the relationship with their mothers. They retained no memory of telling their mother not to kiss them. Decades later, they were simply anguished and resentful that she had shown them no affection. The younger generation did not understand any more than their fathers. No one had explained the basic feminist issue of female self-esteem. Assessing his mother and father, a boy could still wonder: 'Why does she "let" him dominate?'. Sons were issuing the same instructions as their fathers but less frequently, and they did so within a social climate which greatly enhanced women's general status. They were also speaking to mothers who mostly had sufficient confidence, as well as conviction, to find ways to show their love anyway. Any real changes in the relationship have been a by-product of changes in women over the last twenty years rather than a conscious attempt by mothers to match changes in rearing daughters by altering their attitudes to sons.

Mothers and sons do share a unique bond for, if masculine conditioning closes down empathy, it does so only progressively. For a brief few years during their son's adolescence through to young manhood, mothers discover the rare and precious experience of a physically mature male who is still emotionally empathetic—the soul mate of every woman's romantic dreams. It ends almost before they have grasped its significance. For many, it is never more than a fleeting glimpse anyway. The son moves off to his adult life. The conditioning takes over and the cycle begins again. His own son will one day wonder why his father cannot tell when he is hurting his mother. Another woman will suffer from lack of empathy in her partner, and blame his mother. Another man will live an emotionally isolated life and wonder why he never quite connects to anyone—or be oblivious to the lack of connection.

The mother–son relationship demonstrates how much men hurt themselves by their definition of masculinity yet, as Andrew Tolson pointed out in *The Limits of Masculinity*, while the process of *achieving* manhood is under constant scrutiny, the goal is never questioned.[75] It is the yardstick for what a man *is* which needs examining. Persisting with a version which is inappropriate in Western society at the end of the twentieth century produces nothing but sorrow for both men and women. It comprises ideas of masculinity which were suitable to tribal society centuries ago and which were constructed on fundamental power relationships arising from physical size and strength. These are not only superfluous but frequently destructive in contemporary terms.

Author Heather Formaini interviewed 120 men. She was struck by the widespread sense of inadequacy.

> Of all the many men I interviewed and of all the men I see in therapy, not one of them feels himself to be masculine. They feel as though they are failures because they don't measure up to what they believe masculine men ought to be.[76]

The likely solution will be similar to that for women—loosen up the definition of masculinity. Allow for variety. And relax in the freedom from pressure which will result. Men, too, could develop variations on what constitutes a 'proper' man. And, in a world where masculine identity was less fragile, where men could be confident in their maleness and not so easily threatened, there would also be room for homosexual males to be accepted as being different, but not lesser, men.

The reappraisal of masculinity must be a male initiative. Women do not have a mortgage on wisdom about human identity, nor a monopoly on feelings. It is possible to be as unbalanced by excessive emotion as it is by too little—objectivity is as valuable as subjectivity. There are many masculine qualities which should be celebrated, not least, as any mother of a growing boy can attest, the sheer physicality of young males—their size, strength, energy—and their enthusiasm, affection and the serious purpose which can lurk beneath the bravado. They need new heroes to emulate, masculine models that are admirable and worthy of respect because they demonstrate how to function in the contemporary world. If they can find none, then the generation who are presently still teenagers will, ultimately, proceed to redefine 'masculinity' in their own image. The insight and co-operation of their forebears would hasten the process—and reduce the risk.

Lack of change in concepts of masculinity has played a major role in limiting change in the mother–son relationship. It has also left mothers with a lonely struggle to generate respect and admiration from their sons. It is crucial that women understand the forces arrayed against them. If a mother does not hold her son responsible for the consequences of his actions; if she acts softly feminine instead of womanly tough; if, in the time-honoured female way, she protects his masculine ego by putting herself down or taking his blame; if she doesn't stand up to him with quiet assurance; if she feels guilty, or apologises for just being around—for intruding her motherly presence into his masculine world—she should not for one moment think that he will understand and applaud her unselfishness. These are boys not girls. In a boy's world, the applause goes to the brave and the confident and the strong. Self-sacrifice is weakness. It is also everything he is trying not to be—girlish.

Masculinity may have resisted change, but the transformation in women has altered the core dynamics in the relationship anyway. Contemporary mothers and sons are not always more equal, but most are far more friendly. And the friendship of mothers who are active, worldly, mentally flexible and curious people should have a major influence in the way that sons view women generally. The 'typical' mother might develop a multifaceted dimension and the stereotype of the typical would be less likely to overwhelm the individual. Perhaps then, mothers and sons can resolve their adult relationship. There is a new and positive sign that they will: men who are pioneering more intimate involvement with their children are discovering unexpected insights:

> *Some of my mother's experience in nursing babies has surfaced from some deep memory and I have become parent-in-charge of burps and colic . . . I find it curiously satisfying to recall and use my mother's wisdom. (age 42, son six months)*

Once empowered by a new male perspective, men can allow themselves to love their mothers without ambivalence and abandon the 'mummy's boy' abuse. By taking emotional responsibility for integrating rather than avoiding their mothers in adult life, they will come to recognise that there are no maternal archetypes, that the 'good' mother is an aspiration, not a reality. They can cast out their old maternal targets—the Jewish mother, the Italian mumma, the American mom, the intrusive mother, the possessive mother, the seductive mother . . . Society has gained much pleasure from deriding these stereotypes but now, when we laugh at them, we should also weep. There are patterns in the bonds between mothers and sons, but not 'types'. Only real people. They are individual relationships springing from specific personal circumstances, from past anxieties or present needs, from a variety of human qualities—all different. They are not, and never should be, labelled 'stereotypes'. Rather, we should look for the human beings concealed by the caricatures, considering their shortcomings with fellowship and, at all times, with 'the eye of pity' for, as Virgil discovered centuries ago: 'These are the tears of things and the human condition touches the soul'.[77]

Notes

1 Llewellyn Jones, Derek, *Everyman*, p. 40.
2 Bly, Robert, *Iron John*, pp. 86–7.
3 Stoltenberg, John, *Refusing to be a Man*, p. 80.
4 Tolson, Andrew, *The Limits of Masculinity*, p. 25.
5 Steinem, Gloria, cover endorsement on *Refusing to be a Man.*
6 'The Changing Role of the Male', Summary Report of the Working Party for Ministry of Labour, Sweden, 1986 pp. 19–20.
7 Stoltenberg, op. cit., p. 198 & Preface.
8 Kagan, Jerome, in H. Wilmer, *Mothers/Fathers*, p. 75.
9 Wylie, Phillip, *A Generation of Vipers*, 1955 ed.
10 Adler, D.L. 'Matriduxy in the Australian Family', in Davies, A.F. and Encel, S., *Australian Society*, p. 149.
11 Friedan, B., *The Feminine Mystique*, p. 165.
12 Rich, Adrienne, *Of Woman Born*, p. 196.
13 Friedan, B. op. cit., pp. 165–6.
14 Martin, Jean I., 'Marriage, The Family and Class', in *Marriage and the Family in Australia*', (ed.) A.P. Elkin, p. 33.
15 Browne, Sheila, 'Old Sayings Never Die', *Sydney Morning Herald*, 17 November 1992.
16 ibid.
17 McElwain, D.W. and Campbell, W.J., 'The Family', in Davies, A.F. and Encel, S., *Australian Society*, op. cit., p. 148.
18 ibid.

19 Bibring, Greta, cited in Chodorow, Nancy, *The Reproduction of Mothering*, pp. 184–5.
20 Chodorow, Nancy, *The Reproduction of Mothering*, pp. 184–5.
21 Arcana, Judith, 'Every Woman's Son', p. 229
22 Dr John Buttsworth interview with researcher Sherri Stumm, October 1991.
23 'Nursery Crimes', Lyndall Crisp, *The Bulletin*, 20 August 1991, p. 82 and telephone conversation with Professor Kim Oates of Royal Alexandria Hospital for Children, 6 November 1992.
24 Rudi Guerra interview with researcher Sherri Stumm, October 1991.
25 John Buttsworth interview, op. cit.
26 *Sunday Times*, 5 May 1992.
27 Professor Brent Waters, personal interview with researcher Sherri Stumm, October 1991.
28 Rudi Guerra personal interview with researcher Sherri Stumm, October 1991.
29 McMillan, Peter, *Men, Sex and Other Secrets*, p. 47.
30 Whyte, Paul, personal interview with author, Sydney, September 1992.
31 Whyte, Paul, op. cit.
32 Eardley, Tony, in *The Sexuality of Men*, (ed.) Andy Metcalf, pp. 106–7. Refers also to research by Dobash, R.E. and Dobash, R., *Violence Against Wives*, London, Open Books, 1980.
33 Whyte, Paul, op. cit.
34 Green, Toby, interview with researcher, Sherri Stumm, October 1991.
35 Steinem, Gloria, *Revolution From Within: a Book of Self-Esteem*, p. 309.
36 de Vaus, June, *Mothers Growing Up*, pp. 134–5.
37 de Vaus, June, ibid., p. 103.
38 ibid., p. 105.
39 ibid., p. 86.
40 Burrett, Jill, author of *To and Fro Children* interviewed on ABC Radio 'Offspring' programme, 1st July 1991.
41 *Journal of Sex, Marriage and the Family*, vol. 6, no. 1.
42 de Vaus, June, op. cit. Chapter 5 and particularly p. 87.
43 Buttsworth, John, interview with researcher Sherri Stumm, October 1991.
44 Green, Toby, interview with researcher Sherri Stumm, October 1991.
45 de Vaus, June, op. cit., pp. 116–18.
46 ibid., p. 116–18 and referring particularly to Nicholson, *The Heartache of Motherhood*, 1983 and Orbach and Eichenbaum *What do Women Want?*, 1983.

47 Harper, Jan and Richards, Lyn, 'Mothers and Working Mothers', in Bryson, Lois, *The Patriarchal Family*, p. 140.
48 Bryson, Lois, *The Patriarchal Family*, op. cit., p. 140.
49 Personal interview with researcher, Sherry Stumm, Sydney, October 1991.
50 Bittman, Michael, 'Juggling Time: How Australian Families Use Time', Analysis of Statistics for the Office of the Status of Women.
51 Statham, June, *Daughters and Sons*, p. 96.
52 ibid., p. 75.
53 'Attitudes to Marriage among Young Tertiary Educated Women', *Australian Journal of Social Issues*, vol. 24, no. 2, May 1989.
54 Amato, Paul, *Children in Australian Families*, pp. 46–7.
55 Mackay, Hugh, 'The Mackay Report: Australians at Home, 1986', p. 8; Glezer, Helen, 'To tie or not to Tie the Knot: pathways to Family Formation', Australian Family Research Conference, 17–19 February 1993.
56 Mackay, Hugh, 'The Mackay Report: Teenagers and their Parents, 1988', pp. 41–2.
57 Metcalf, Andy, *The Sexuality of Men*, p. 174.
58 'The Women's View': Report commissioned by the Office of the Status of Women, Australia, July–August 1992.
59 Arndt, Bettina, 'The House Divided', *Weekend Australian*, June 27–28, 1992, p. 22.
60 Harmer, Wendy, *The Weekend Australian*, October 12–13, 1991.
61 de Vaus, David, personal correspondence 9 April 1993 concerning his book *Letting Go: relationships between adults and their parents*, to be published by Oxford University Press, Melbourne, 1994.
62 ibid.
63 Correspondence between the author and Leila Friedman, author of *Why Can't I Sleep at Nana's Anymore?*
64 Taylor, Geraldine, personal correspondence 29 May 1992 and 6 June 1992.
65 ibid.
66 ibid.
67 ibid.
68 Greer, Germaine, 'Are Mothers Really Necessary', TV documentary produced and directed by David Pick. A TVS Production.
69 ibid.
70 Ferris, Thelma, personal interview, Sydney 1991.
71 Rich, Adrienne, *Of Woman Born*, p. 246.

72 de Vaus, June, op. cit.
73 ibid.
74 Friedmann, Leila, op. cit.
75 Tolson, Andrew, op.cit.
76 Formaini, Heather, *Men: the darker continent*, p. 8.
77 Virgil, *Aeneid*, Book 1, 1.462.

Selected bibliography

Adler, D.L., 'Matriduxy in the Australian Family', in *Australian Society: A Sociological Introduction*, A.F. Davies and S. Encel (eds), F.W. Cheshire, Melbourne, 1965

Amato, Paul, *Children in Australian Families: the growth of competence*, Prentice-Hall, Sydney, 1987

Ansbacher, H.L. and Ansbacher, R.R. (eds), *The Individual Psychology of Alfred Adler*, Harper & Row, Torchbook edn, New York, 1967

Arcana, Judith, *Every Mother's Son*, The Women s Press, London, 1983

Argyle, Michael and Henderson, Monika, *The Anatomy of Relationships*, Pelican, London, 1988

Arnstein, Helene S., *Between Mothers-in-law and Daughters-in-law: Achieving a successful and caring relationship*, Dodd, Mead & Company, New York, 1985

Bacchi, Carol Lee, *Same Difference*, Allen & Unwin, Sydney, 1990

Beail, Nigel and McGuire, Jacqueline (eds), *Fathers: Psychological Perspectives*, Junction Books, London, 1982. (Contributors: Judy Blendis, Bedford College, London, 'Men's Experiences of Their Own Fathers'; Jacqueline McGuire, Thomas Coram Research Unit, University of London, 'Gender Specific Differences in Early Childhood: The Impact of the Father'; Charlie Lewis, Susan Isaacs Research Fellow, Child Development Research Unit, University of Nottingham, Elizabeth Newson and John Newson, Child Development Research Unit, University of Nottingham, 'Father Participation Through Childhood and its Relationship with Career Aspirations and Delinquency'.)

Bell, Donald H., *Being a Man: the paradox of masculinity*, The Lewis Publishing Company, Mass. USA, 1982

Bittman, Michael, 'Juggling Time: How Australian Families Use Time', Secondary Analysis of 1987 Pilot Survey of Time Use, prepared for Office of the Status of Women, CPN Publications Pty Limited, May 1991

Bly, Robert, *Iron John*, Element Books Limited, Dorset, 1992

Bryson, Lois, 'The Australian Patriarchal Family', in *Australian Society: Sociological Essays*, 4th edn, S. Encel and L. Bryson, eds, Longman Cheshire, Melbourne, 1984

Burns, Ailsa and Goodnow, Jacqueline, *Children and Families in Australia*, in *Studies in Society: Contemporary Issues and Problems*, George Allen & Unwin, Sydney, 1979

Burrett, Jill, *To and Fro Children: A Guide to Successful Parenting after Divorce*, Allen & Unwin, Sydney, 1991

Chesler, Phyllis, *About Men*, The Women's Press, London, 1979

Chodorow, Nancy, *The Reproduction of Mothering*, University of California Press, Berkeley, 1978

Collange, Christiane, *I'm Your Mother*, tr. Helen McPhail, Gillian Willy, (ed.), Arrow Books, London, 1987

Collings, Terry, *Beyond Mateship*, Simon & Schuster, Sydney, 1992

Collings, Terry and Vickers, Janet, *Teenagers: a guide to understanding them*, Bantam, Sydney, 1988

Connell, W.F. et.al., 'Growing Up in an Australian City: a study of Adolescents in Sydney', Australian Council for Educational Research, Australia, 1959

Davies, A.F. and Encel, S., *Australian Society: a sociological introduction*, F.W. Cheshire, Melbourne, 1965

de Vaus, David, *Letting Go: relationships between adults and their parents*, Oxford University Press, Melbourne, 1994

de Vaus, June E., *Mothers Growing Up: understanding the heartaches of motherhood*, Allen & Unwin, Sydney, 1992

Dinnerstein, Dorothy, *The rocking of the cradle and the ruling of the world*, The Women's Press, London, 1987

Dixson, Miriam, *The Real Matilda: Women and Identity in Australia 1788 to the present*, Penguin Australia, revised edition, 1983

Dowrick, S. and Grundberg, S. (eds), *Why Children?*, The Women's Press, London, 1980

Eardley, Tony, in *The Sexuality of Men*, Andy Metcalf and Martin Humphries (eds), Pluto Press, London and Sydney, 1985

Eichenbaum, L. and Orbach, S., *What Do Women Want?*, Michael Joseph Ltd, London, 1983

SELECTED BIBLIOGRAPHY

Elkin, A.P., (ed.), *Marriage and the Family in Australia*, Angus & Robertson, Sydney, 1957

Eysenck, Hans, *Decline and Fall of the Freudian Empire*, Pelican Books, Harmondsworth, 1986

Ford, Anna, *Men: A documentary*, Weidenfeld and Nicholson, London, 1985

Formaini, Heather, *Men: the darker continent*, William Heinemann Ltd, Melbourne, 1990

Franks, Helen, *Goodbye Tarzan: Men after feminism*, George Allen & Unwin, London & Sydney, 1984

Friedan, Betty, *The Feminine Mystique*, Penguin Books, Ringwood, 1963

——*The Second Stage*, Michael Joseph Ltd., London, 1982

Frosh, Stephen, *The Politics of Psychoanalysis: An introduction to Freudian and Post-Freudian Theory*, Macmillan Education Ltd, London, 1987

Gieve, Katherine, (ed.), *Balancing Acts: On Being a Mother*, Virago, London 1989

Glezer, Helen, 'To Tie or not to Tie the Knot: pathways to Family Formation', Australian Family Research Conference, 17–19 February 1993

Greer, Germaine, *The Female Eunuch*, Granada Publishing, London, 1971

Grieve, Norma and Perdices, Michael, 'Patriarchy: a refuge from maternal power? Dinnerstein's answer to Freud', in Grieve, N. and Grimshaw, P. (eds), *Australian Women: Feminist Perspectives*, Oxford University Press, Melbourne, 1981

Harper, Jan and Richard, Lyn, *Mothers and Working Mothers*, Penguin, Ringwood, 1979

Hewlett, Sylvia Ann, *A Lesser Life: the myth of Women's Liberation*, Michael Joseph Ltd, London, 1987

Hite, Shere, *The Hite Report: Women and Love*, Penguin Books, Ringwood, 1989

——, *The Hite Report on Male Sexuality*, Macdonald, Sydney, 1978

Johnson, Robert A., *HE: understanding masculine psychology*, Harper & Row, Perennial Library, New York, 1986

Johnson, Miriam M., *Strong Mothers, Weak Wives: the search for gender equality*, University of California Press, Berkeley, 1988

Kagan, Jerome, *The Nature of the Child*, Basic Books, New York, 1984, cited in *Mother/Father*, Harry A. Wilmer (ed.), Chiron Pubs, Illinois, 1990

Llewellyn-Jones, Derek, *Everyman*, Oxford University Press, Oxford, 1991

McElwain, D.W. and Campbell, W.J., 'The Family', in *Australian Society: A Sociological Introduction*, A.F. Davies and S. Encel (eds), F.W. Cheshire, Melbourne, 1965

Mackay, Hugh, 1983 'The Mackay Report: The Working Wife', Mackay Research, Bathurst NSW

——, 1986 'The Mackay Report: Australians at Home', Bathurst NSW

——, 1988 'The Mackay Report: Teenagers and Their Parents', Mackay Research, Chatswood NSW

——, 1989 'The Mackay Report: Men and Women', Mackay Research, Chatswood, NSW

——, 1993 *Reinventing Australia,* Collins Angus & Robertson, Sydney

McMillan, Peter, *Men, Sex and Other Secrets,* The Text Publishing Company, Melbourne, 1992

Maloney, Mercedes Lynch and Maloney, Anne, *The Hand That Rocks the Cradle: Mothers, Sons and leadership,* Prentice-Hall, New Jersey, 1985

Martin, Jean I., 'Marriage, The Family and Class', in *Marriage and the Family in Australia,* ed. A.P. Elkin, Angus and Robertson, Sydney, 1957

Metcalf, Andy and Humphries, Martin (eds), *The Sexuality of Men,* Pluto Press, London & Sydney, 1985

Miles, Rosalind, 'The Rites of Man: Love, Sex and Death', in *The Making of the Male,* Grafton Books, a division of HarperCollins, London, 1991

Nathan, Joel, *Time of my life,* Penguin Books, Ringwood, 1992

Nicholson, Joyce, *The Heartache of Motherhood,* Penguin Books, Ringwood, 1983

Olivier, Christiane, *Jocasta's Children: the imprint of the mother,* tr. George Craig, Routledge, London, 1990

Orgler, Hertha, *Alfred Adler, The Man and His Work: Triumph over the Inferiority Complex,* rev. edn, Sidgwick & Jackson, London, 1973

Phillips, Shelley, *Beyond the Myths: mother–daughter relationships,* Hampden Press, Sydney, 1991

Rich, Adrienne, *Of Woman Born: Motherhood as Experience and Institution,* Virago, London, 1977

Roberts, Yvonne, *Man Enough: men of 35 speak out,* Chatto & Windus, The Hogarth Press, London, 1984

Royal Commission on Human Relationships, Final Report, vol. 4, pt. 5, 'The Family: Evidence', Australian Government Publishing Service, Canberra, 1977

Russell, Graeme, *The Changing Role of Fathers?,* University of Queensland Press, St Lucia, 1983

Statham, June, *Daughters and Sons: Experiences of non-sexist childraising,* Basil Blackwell Ltd, Oxford & New York, 1986

Steinem, Gloria, *Revolution from Within: a book of self-esteem,* Corgi Books, London, 1992

Stoltenberg, John, *Refusing to be a Man,* Fontana/Collins, London, 1990

SELECTED BIBLIOGRAPHY

Summary of the Report of the Swedish Ministry of Labour into 'The Changing Role of the Male', David Knight & Co., Sweden, 1986

Summers, Anne, *Damned Whores and God's Police: The Colonization of Women in Australia*, Penguin, Ringwood, 1975

'The Women's View', report commissioned by the Office of the Status of Women, Australia, July–August, 1992

Thompson, Keith (ed.), *Views from the Male World*, The Aquarian Press, a HarperCollins imprint, London, 1992

Tolson, Andrew, *The Limits of Masculinity*, 1977 Tavistock Publications Limited, London, 1982 edn

Wearing, Betsy, *The Ideology of Motherhood: a study of Sydney suburban mothers*, George Allen & Unwin, Sydney, 1984

Wilmer, Harry (ed.), *Mother/Father*, Chiron Publications, Illinois, 1990

Winn, Denise, *Men on Divorce*, Piatkus Ltd, London, 1986

Wylie, Philip, *A Generation of Vipers*, Frederick Muller Ltd, London, 1955

Periodicals

Australian Journal of Social Issues, vol. 24, no. 2, May 1989, 'Attitudes to Marriage among Young Tertiary Educated Women', Ailsa Burns and Cath Scott

Journal of Child Abuse and Neglect, 1989, vol. 13, 'Adult Male Report of Childhood Sexual Abuse by Mothers: Case Descriptions, Motivations and Long-term Consequences', Ronald S. Krug